PULL YOUR NOSE UP

The Insurance Agent's Flight Manual For
Correcting Course And Gaining Altitude

Anthony D. Cefalu

AuthorHouse™
1663 Liberty Drive
Bloomington, IN 47403
www.authorhouse.com
Phone: 1-800-839-8640

© 2011 Anthony D. Cefalu. All rights reserved.

No part of this book may be reproduced, stored in
a retrieval system, or transmitted by any means
without the written permission of the author.

First published by AuthorHouse 4/11/2011

ISBN: 978-1-4567-4080-1 (sc)
ISBN: 978-1-4567-4079-5 (e)

Library of Congress Control Number: 2011904884

Printed in the United States of America

Any people depicted in stock imagery provided by Thinkstock are models,
and such images are being used for illustrative purposes only.
Certain stock imagery © Thinkstock.

This book is printed on acid-free paper.

Because of the dynamic nature of the Internet, any web addresses or
links contained in this book may have changed since publication and
may no longer be valid. The views expressed in this work are solely those
of the author and do not necessarily reflect the views of the publisher,
and the publisher hereby disclaims any responsibility for them.

"This second book of Tony's shows the intricacies of owning and operating your business with great precision. You'll learn what to do, why to do it and how to accomplish your production goals. By employing the techniques in this book you'll find yourself going to the next level in your career because of the value of these sales ideas, advice, marketing tips. Keep your highlighter handy; you'll want to quickly reference back to Tony's book time and again."

Katrina Botimer, Insurance & Financial Services Agent

"Pull Your Nose Up' is chock full of useful ideas and information for the insurance and financial services professional in particular. Follow the advice and principles Tony shares in this book and you will be successful; guaranteed."

Tim Allen, MSF, Agency General Manager

"I believe my fellow sales professionals will enjoy reading "Pull Your Nose Up" and find Tony's insights valuable. Following his advice should improve sales performance regardless of your level of experience and expertise. Small business owners will find benefit because this book provides simple, straightforward ideas that work! Although I already see eye-to-eye with Tony, as I read this book, I became excited about ways to continue to improve my own performance!"

Beth Trotter, Agency Sales Manager

"If you are looking for a useful book to read with meaningful ideas to improve your sales results, 'Pull Your Nose Up' is the one for you. It's an easy book to read...not presumptuous or falsely intellectual. Instead, this is a very practical book with a lot of great ideas and the results to prove it."

Sarah Thompson, Agency Training Consultant

"Tony has done it again, 'Pull Your Nose Up', is a welcome addition to his first work, 'Sales Is a Contact Sport'. This book is a reference book, an idea book, a tool for the sales professional who wants to get back on track and stay there...It's a practical book as well; worth the money and time to read. I highly recommend it."

Jim Anderson, Founder & Owner, Endless Computers

"This book is packed with great ideas on how to improve, maintain, and re-motivate any sales professional. I recommend this book as a required reading for anyone in business for themselves or experience the pressure of making a commission. In addition, this book should be re-read several times in order to recapture the fundamentals of sales which many professionals lack or forget over the course of time."

Shauna Spence, Agent, Health & Life

"Practical, useful, full of ideas and advice on how to be a better sales professional and business owner. Every agent, new and seasoned, should read this book to stay fresh and to jump start their production results."

Tim Thompson, Insurance & Financial Services Agency Owner

"...highly recommended reading, particularly for the sales professional who is 'stuck' and looking for new ideas and new energy to get their business operation moving in the right direction. Tony puts things into their proper perspective and provides practical advice to give any business professional an edge in a competitve marketplace."

Brian Feuer, Team Ohio Financial Advisors LLC, Owner/President

"If you want to really reach and understand your clients and become a real professional--not just a pitch expert--check out Cefalu's book. His experience and practical wisdom is evident and the Value Diamond Concept has a ring of truth you won't be able to ignore."

Dasaya Cates, Author and Blogger

This book is dedicated to all the agents and staff team members with whom I have had the privilege of working. It has been a pleasure to be part of their professional and personal success.

Preface

Pull Your Nose Up is a companion work to my first book, *Sales Is a Contact Sport*, in which the psychological motives of the customer and their mechanism for buying are explored.

"Pull your nose up" is a common aviation expression typically used as a warning to a pilot of impending collision due to a loss of altitude or as an instructive command when teaching about a particular aerial maneuver or course correction. As a former Air Force officer familiar with flying and all types of airframes, I can see some of the parallels that can be drawn between the responsibilities and challenges of being in command of a fighter aircraft and being responsible and in command of a small business.

There are, admittedly, distinct characteristics between the two that make the parallel far from exact, and it is not my aim to diminish or minimize the life-and-death consequences faced daily by our men and women in uniform so that we can live free. I am a war veteran myself and have the deepest respect for those who voluntarily choose to serve and protect this great country of ours. Bearing this in mind, I must say, "Thank you for answering the call of duty in defense of America. I am indebted to you."

I also know that any rational small business owner would agree that the challenges they face in the marketplace as civilians cannot begin to compare to the sacrifices and challenges those serving in the military have to overcome. So, in utilizing the expression

"Pull your nose up" as the title for this book, it is my intention to help the small business owner—particularly the agency owner who sells insurance—to avoid some of the common pitfalls akin to running a business.

The harsh reality is that many agency owners selling insurance and financial services are 'nose down', heading for the ground. For some, the ground is still some distant doom, obscured by the clouds, but unbeknownst to them, the ground is approaching fast. For others who are not sure how to read their instrument panels, everything looks just fine. But the indicators are there! The instruments don't lie, and the danger is real and imminent. The warning to "Pull your nose up" must be heeded, or a crash of financial proportions is going to occur.

But how does it happen? How does a business owner who starts out with all the will and grit and brains needed to be successful end up losing 'altitude', so to speak, in the marketplace to eventually end up closing the doors to business in the end, crashing into the ground of failure in a catastrophic financial mess? The answer to this question is that there are many reasons such a tragedy occurs.

In a plane, a downward glide might be due to spatial disorientation, loss of perspective and orientation, or loss of situational awareness, leading to disaster for a pilot. I think the same can be said for the agent-owner who experiences a 'loss of altitude' in their business.

This book is, therefore, written for the agent-owner who has possibly lost perspective in the marketplace and/or an awareness of the competitive environment that threatens to cause a business 'crash'. Where your 'nose' is pointed matters; every pilot knows this, and every agent-owner should apply the same realization to their business operation.

If you are a business owner or an agent-owner, think of this book as a 'flight manual', of sorts, designed to help you pull your nose up and keep your agency aloft and flying higher than ever.

Are you losing altitude in your business? Are your instruments warning you of impending crash? When the visible signs are there, explore the lessons and advice contained in this flight manual to regain your business and financial altitude. It will help you make the necessary corrections in your agency's flight path, allowing you to soar to higher profits and greater personal success.

The key is to pull your nose up… and these pages will show you how!

Contents

Preface vii

All Customers Are Created Equal, but Some are
More Equal than Others 1

How Disturbing Are You to People? 3

You Cannot Out-Perform Your Own Self-Image. 11

The Pain of Discipline or the Pain of Regret. 21

$E = MC^2$: A New Theory of Relativity 23

Experience is NOT the Best Teacher 25

Successful People Know Their Numbers. 41

Psychological Reciprocity 45

To Make Them Thirsty, Make the Well Run Dry 47

Brief Is Better 51

Stupid Things I've Heard & What I Think When I
Hear Them... 53

The Difference. 57

It Does Matter Who You Know 59

The Whole Package 65

Be Brilliant at the Basics 83

Make the Best of the First Seven Seconds.............. 89

You Are the Missing Link 95

Success Is the Best Revenge. 101

How Often Has this Happened to You?. 105

Hire for the Position, Not the Person 109

You Are Not Responsible for Results.................. 117

Slow to Hire, Quick to Fire 125

Off to a Good Start, But with No End in Sight......... 127

Don't Be a Half-Brained Sales Professional 131

No One Will Have Done You a Favor by Buying from You 137

The Key to an Effective Close is a Powerful Opening... 143

Principles Endure, and Methodologies Vary 151

When Great Customer Service Can Kill Your Business . 155

Claim Day is Game Day 159

Paralyzed by Perfection............................ 165

Be Deliberately Successful.......................... 169

Ideas Are a Dime a Dozen, But Their Execution is Priceless.. 175

Fail Your Failures Fast & Other Talent Acquisition & Management Principles......................... 179

Create a Detailed Staff Team Handbook & Job Description 187

Hire Attitude-Aptitude-Appearance 189

Expectations and Outcomes........................ 191

Don't Fall in Love and Other Words-of-Wisdom 195

To Diet or Not to Diet? 201

Control Your Calendar Before It Controls You 207

Game Maker...Or Game Breaker.................... 215

Gone Without a Complaint 221

Don't Boil the Ocean 225

All Customers Are Created Equal, but Some are More Equal than Others

I've been criticized by many sales professionals for declaring openly that "All customers are created equal—but some are more equal than others."

Somehow, it is construed I unfairly favor one group of customers over another. Well, the fact that I am biased toward certain customers versus other customers is true, but I am not biased unfairly.

What I am simply trying to state to business people, sales professionals, and entrepreneurs is that <u>every</u> customer has an economic value to your business or profession. This economic value can be prioritized or graded. In the case of the sales professional running a sales organization or agency, every customer and every separate account brings unequal amounts of revenue into your business.

Therefore, I am merely stating a fact of economics. Those customers or accounts which bring me the most revenue value get treated differently than those who bring in less revenue value relative to my efforts. This isn't professional heresy; it is just prudent business practice.

Now, please understand I am not advocating that certain customers get treated well while others get treated poorly. All customers deserve a good experience, respect, attention, care, and professional service, and all desire to get their money's worth, as they deserve.

The message is this: With the limited time we have each working day to invest in people along with the finite monetary resources available for marketing and selling, the smart sales professional favors expenditure of these valuable assets (time and money) on those customers who are most valuable to the business enterprise.

It doesn't make sense on a business level to weight precious resources in favor of customers who do not have the greater weight of economic benefit to the agency.

Prioritize your customer list and accounts. Treat all customers as if they are the most important person when you are transacting business with them, but when marketing resources come into question or a decision has to be made as to where sales dollars are spent, remember, "Some customers are more equal than others."

How Disturbing Are You to People?

One of the most renowned insurance salesmen to have ever lived was Ben Feldman from East Liverpool, Ohio, a small, low-income community situated in the northeast part of the state. East Liverpool and the surrounding communities are populated, by the most part, with blue collar residents.

In his day, Feldman wrote more life insurance in one year than some insurance companies did. During his lifetime, he wrote over $1 billion in life insurance and was recognized by the *Guinness Book of World Records* as the "most outstanding salesman in history."

When someone of Feldman's caliber speaks, people should listen. According to Feldman, a key to his success was his courage to ask his prospects what he called "the disturbing questions." That is, he asked his prospects well-thought-out, planned questions that were purposefully designed to reveal their underlying need or desire for protection. Although his expertise was in the life insurance realm, his methods and salesmanship techniques apply to our efforts as multiline agents.

Feldman's "disturbing questions" are the kind of questions that trigger the emotions and disturb a person into thinking about circumstances they would normally not consider on their own. It's a means of provoking thought and bringing about clarity on those issues of life that can easily and suddenly turn someone's world upside down. That's your challenge. That's your job... and I might add, it's also your responsibility and obligation as a professional.

Feldman understood how people think. He knew people don't move in their minds from "I have a problem" to "I have a need for your product and service" until they are first made to consider the consequences of the problem and personalize them, relating them to their own lives.

UNTIL A THING BECOMES RELEVANT, IT HAS NO IMPORTANCE

Consider the following disturbing questions and build on these when formulating your own disturbing questions game plan!

DISTURBING QUESTIONS ABOUT LONG-TERM HOSPITALIZATION & INABILITY TO WORK:

"Who do you know who has ever suffered from a serious medical problem or has been injured, requiring a significant amount of medical care? When was the last time someone in your family was medically confined due to illness or an accident? What happened? Were you left with bills that were not covered by your medical coverage? What kind of expenses were you left to pay out of your own pocket, medical and otherwise? What did you do? Where did the money come from? How did that make you feel? How helpful would it have been to have had a way to pay those bills without having to pay for them out of pocket? What kind of red tape did you have to deal with when it came to your medical bills? How much wasn't covered? How would you pay for deductibles and co-pays?"

OR

"Imagine you have been struck ill—a stroke or injury to your back while lifting a supply box onto the conveyor belt where you work at XYZ Company. Consider all the expenses not covered by your

Pull Your Nose Up

major medical plan, like deductibles, travel expenses, lodging and rent, meals, prescriptions, and co-pays. How will you pay for these things when that happens? Who is going to help you with paying the bills? How will you be able to meet your mortgage and utilities and still pay for gas in the car or put food on the table? When I don't work, I don't get paid. What happens when you can't work due to illness or accident? How will it affect your family? What will they do? What considerations should be made in case you become sick or injured and cannot earn a paycheck? What will happen? How will you manage? How will your family feel or react if the bills go unpaid because of the extra expenses incurred as a result of your illness or injury? How will being unable to work due to injury or illness affect your ability to pay for your debts, bills, monthly obligations, deductibles, and co-pays?"

DISTURBING QUESTIONS ABOUT LONG-TERM CARE, NURSING HOMES & MEDICAID:

"What plans have you made to protect your assets? What plans have you made to make sure your children will inherit your assets? What plans have you made to prevent having to live in a nursing facility when your health declines? Has anyone ever explained to you to your satisfaction what happens when Medicaid is used for long-term care? Who do you want to inherit your home, your savings? How would you feel if your family has to give your home and other assets to the government to pay for your care and your Medicaid benefits? Do you know anyone who has needed long-term care? How familiar are you with what happens when nursing home care is needed and how it is paid for or not paid for? How did it change their lives and affect them? What financial burdens did they experience? When your health fails, would you rather have a plan in place that gives you control over your care, or are you content to be at the mercy of your condition? What are your plans for when your health changes? Do you plan to live with your children when your health changes? How will that work? How do your children feel about it? What kind of burdens would that add to their family situation? How do you feel about the possibilities of having to live with your children if you were to need continuous care? When your health changes, would you like to remain in your home and have in-home care? Why? How will you make sure that happens, that you have that option? Where will the money come from? How will it affect you if you cannot live at home anymore? How important will it be for you to maintain the control and choice over your healthcare in the future? How would you feel if someone else was in control of your medical care and the choices you have for assisted care? When you are no longer able to care for yourself, what is going to happen? Who will take care of you?"

DISTURBING QUESTIONS ABOUT LIFE INSURANCE:

"If you were to die today, Mark, how would your wife Melissa and little Mark and little Melissa maintain the standard of living you've worked so hard to provide for them? How would the mortgage get paid? How would the utilities and all those other bills like food, clothes, and car upkeep be provided for if you are no longer around to earn a living for them? How tragic would it be for them to live, struggling constantly to make ends meet, and maintain their own self-respect when it comes to being responsible and paying their bills? How would Melissa feel if she had to take just any job to make sure the bills get paid? Where would the money come from for little Mark and little Melissa to go to college as you've said you want them to? What would happen to their dreams and hopes if they aren't able to go to college?"

DISTURBING QUESTIONS ABOUT AUTO INSURANCE:

"Mark, let's say you are driving down Main Street and accidentally swerve the car—for one reason or another—and go left of center on the roadway, hitting another vehicle head-on. If the other driver was hurt badly and needed hospitalization, they might sue you. What would you do, Mark, if you were sued? How would you pay for it? What would you do if your savings, 401k, and other assets like your inheritance or your children's college funds were suddenly at risk of being seized by the courts in settlement of the

damages claimed against you for hurting and injuring the other driver?"

These are just some simple examples of how a sales conversation might sound. We can debate on the strength of the disturbing questions and scenarios I offer here as examples, but don't let that distract you from the point being presented. And that point is to *be disturbing*—to be compelling and courageous in getting customers to face the possibilities and the realities of life when bad things happen to good people.

It's important to be nice, but do not be nice to a fault. Failing to get customers thinking about the things that can happen if they aren't properly insured is part of our mission and responsibility as insurance professionals. Be disturbing! Ask disturbing questions of your customers and your friends who need auto insurance and life insurance. They may squirm in their seats for a moment, but customers will thank and respect you if they ever need your help or the protection they've purchased from you.

Not long ago, my good friend passed away of a disease that was gradually debilitating to his body and mind. Watching how the disease progressed and overcame him was heartbreaking to witness. My friend was a wonderful individual, one in a million, and I had great respect for him. Our families were close and we had a lot of fun times together. As his diseased advanced, I saw how he slowly drifted away mentally and physically.

Just two years before his diagnosis, our families were enjoying a picnic together, and I mentioned that he might want to consider life insurance for his wife and two beautiful little girls. It was a conversation we had had a dozen times before, but to no avail. I tried to explain to him the importance of making sure his wife and girls were taken care of in case something happened to him, but I wasn't getting through to him.

He often responded lightheartedly, "God will take care of us."

My response was always, "That's true, but sometimes we have to give God something to work with," and that made him laugh. Then I said, "How are your girls going to go to college if you die? What is going to happen to this home when you're gone? What is your wife going to do for money? Right now, she works at home. Surely, without you, she will have to go out and find a traditional job to earn a consistent paycheck. Doesn't she want to be able to stay at home with the girls?"

After I asked enough of the disturbing questions, my friend finally bought a policy, albeit a bit reluctantly. It was a start, something he could build upon when he had more money and was more financially secure. I was a bit relieved, and so was his wife.

Just before he died, we had a private conversation at his bedside. My friend never cried; he was a tough guy, and crying just wasn't his style. In fact, we would kid around about his 'no crying' policy all the time, laughing and accusing him of being a softhearted guy at the core and how he was just trying to hide it by acting macho. He was tough on the outside, with a soft, kind hearted center.

As I sat at his bedside, he said to me with tears in his eyes, "Thank you. Thank you for shaming me into buying that life insurance. Now the girls and my wife will be able to pay the house off. My wife will have to go to work, but at least she won't have to worry about the mortgage. That's a big deal, Tony. Thanks for being my friend."

He died not long after that conversation. I miss him, and I know his family does as well, but he did the right thing for them. He didn't leave them empty handed, with sleepless nights filled with worry about how the bills will get paid. He left a legacy to carry on.

In this case, I was speaking to a friend, someone I had a good relationship with and who I felt I had the liberty to do some straight talking with, disturbing him as to the possible consequences of what will happen without adequate life insurance to pay for the bills. Maybe it was easier to have courage talking to a friend, but

Pull Your Nose Up

I have had that same difficult conversation with many people during my career. I have been *disturbing* people for years!

I have other stories chronicling the miracle of life insurance, but his is the most memorable for me, and I'm happy to have *disturbed* him—or, as he said, "shamed" him—persuading him into buying what he needed for his family. Hopefully, you would do the same.

"How disturbing are you to people?" I hope the answer is that you are very disturbing, because in the end, it's the one annoyance people can't live without.

You Cannot Out-Perform Your Own Self-Image

Knowledge about people and a fundamental understanding of the dynamics of how behavior and one's thinking are inextricably linked together are valuable assets for the sales expert. This knowledge can spell the difference between being a great salesperson and a not-so-great salesperson, and it will likely show up in the numbers.

Even though there are some inherently universal, underlying personality traits among people, such as our natural tendency to be judgmental, people are still very different and very, very interesting when we examine individual behavior.

Nevertheless, one of the most constructive lessons I have learned as a sales professional is a one not focused on the customer themselves, but focused on me as a professional in the insurance and financial services industry.

The power of understanding how self-image ties into individual behavior, personal results and outcomes, and a person's likelihood for success in life is one of the greatest and most valuable sales lessons that can be learned.

Anthony D. Cefalu

I AM NOT A PSYCHIATRIST, BUT I DO PLAY ONE AT WORK FROM TIME TO TIME

I am not a revisionist historian, nor do I blame my parents (or anyone, for that matter) for my current faults, failures, and imperfections in life. Yes, I come equipped with all the standard human weaknesses, fears, psychological worries, and imagined boundaries that the next person possesses. In fact, my family and those who know me best on a personal level would probably say I come fully equipped with all the extras when it comes to the psychological baggage that human beings can imagine for themselves.

But, in my maturation and development, I also understand that when past circumstances have been less than favorable for me, ultimately the interpretation of those circumstances and whether or not they produce positive or negative results remains a personal choice nonetheless. Environment and personal choice play large roles in shaping our futures and our outcomes.

In developing this thought about self-image and the connection it has to actual real-world performance results as a professional and as a person, I think it is helpful to be truthful about some of my own personal experiences and resultant thinking and outcomes.

WHAT YOU THINK IS WHO YOU ARE

The connection between our individual experiences and circumstances and what we think of them directly affects outcomes for us. What we think is what we are. As I said, I am not a revisionist historian who blames others and their parents for my problems in life. My parents did a fine job raising us. But in sharing with you my revelations into the power of self-image, I begin with a story about my father.

Born in the 1930's, my father was of a resilient, self-reliant generation. He was a brilliant man, able to work with his hands to build a home or fix plumbing and electrical problems, or just as easily solve the Sunday crossword or managing one of the many businesses he was involved in. He had a college degree, worked as a professional within the parole and penitentiary systems, tried his hand at acting, and was gregarious—the kind of individual who could work with both his hands and his mind. He was truly an extraordinarily talented man.

My father was also a disciplinarian, prone to being somewhat overly critical at times. It was just his way when it came to dealing with his children, and I don't fault him for it. In fact, it can be said that Dad's style created a mental toughness, of sorts, that has stuck with me even to today. That said, it was also the reason I adopted some other not-so-beneficial ways of thinking.

I recall one day when I was about seven years old. Dad was working on the furnace in the basement. I was there watching him, ready and eager to help if he asked for anything. At some point, Dad had asked me to hand him a tool; I'm not too sure what exactly it was that he had asked for, but in any event, I handed him the wrong thing. His reaction was less than approving; let's say it was one of his overly critical moments for me.

In the aftermath of his disapproval, I remember thinking, "Dad is really good with his hands, but I am not." I thought, "I'll never be a man of the Earth like him." That is, I thought I could never be handy like him or able to build and fix things using my hands. After all, I handed him the wrong tool that day, so surely I was bad at using my hands for such things. "Instead," I decided, "I'll be an academic—book smart instead of street smart."

And that's how I grew up. At every turn, I contracted at the thought of taking shop class in high school, and as an adult, I dreaded the thought of fixing something in the house or putting together something as simple as a Christmas bicycle. The words 'household maintenance' were about as appealing to me as having a root canal. It was unpleasant to think I would have to do something that involved fixing, building, or having to use my hands. I just couldn't do it—or at least that is what I thought.

Anthony D. Cefalu

YOU CANNOT OUT-PERFORM YOUR OWN SELF-IMAGE

Fast forward to when I was twenty-eight years old and my wife told me the garbage disposal at home was no longer working. Being the can-do kind of man I thought I was at the time, I did the one thing any red-blooded, self-reliant man would do: I called a plumber.

When Mr. Fix-it came to the house, I showed him to the sink where the broken garbage disposal was and then I proceeded to walk away to let him do his work undisturbed. No sooner had I turned did he advise me that the job was done and the garbage disposal was fixed. I said, "What? Already? How can that be?"

He then showed me the reset button located at the base of the garbage disposal, a trip-fuse that was meant to pop out and shut the disposal unit off in the event the tines within the disposal got jammed by a spoon or a fork, or—God forbid—a finger. The garbage disposal hadn't stopped working; it had just functioned exactly as it had been built to do because in the event of a jam, if the fuse didn't shut the disposal off, it would likely overheat and burn out, causing a fire or permanent damage to the disposal itself. In essence, I called a plumber because my garbage disposal worked exactly like it was supposed to, a safety feature I was completely unaware of.

After paying the fifty bucks to the plumber for the service call and feeling like a total fool, I vowed to never let something like that happen to me again—at least not when it came to the garbage disposal!

Another time, I was considering remodeling the basement in my house to create an entertainment room for watching television and relaxing with visiting friends. Once again, I did the one thing any self-reliant man would do: I called a contractor and got an estimate for the work. The price tag for all the remodeling I wanted done was a shocking $30,000, and I simply didn't have that kind of money to spend.

After I spent several days moping around with my shattered rec room dreams, my wife said to me, "You're a smart guy. Why don't you do it yourself? Call your father and ask him what to do. He'll help you. Go to the library and get some books on how to do the work as well. I know you can do this yourself."

She was right! I did exactly as she suggested, and after a summer of dry wall and sanding, I had successfully remodeled my basement into a proper entertainment center. The cost of the entire do-it-myself project? Less than $5,000—an 80 percent savings over the original contractor estimate.

Lastly, after I separated from the military following the first Gulf War, I started my civilian career with insurance sales.

At the time, I was the sole wage-earner for the family. With two children under three years old, we made the decision that it would be best for my wife to work at home in order to help raise the children while I worked outside the home to build my insurance practice. We rented an apartment at that time and had to budget things very closely since I was starting a new agency and business in a profession that was a complete departure from what we both were accustomed to after nine years in the military.

The car I drove was a used but functional one, albeit the faded paint gave it a very used look. My suits could be described in a similar manner; they weren't used, but they were just plain and a bit out of date, not tailored or fitted like I would have preferred. Money was tight, and as a result, we had to watch every penny very carefully.

SELF-IMAGE DEFINES THE REALM OF THE POSSIBLE

One evening, while driving to an appointment to review an existing policyholder's insurance program, I noticed the neighborhood I was going to had a lot of condominiums in it. As I drove closer to my destination, I saw that the condominiums were not condominiums at all; they were houses—big houses.

I had never met the clients before and had just been recently assigned to their account as the agent-of-record for servicing purposes. The address I pulled into had a long driveway that ended into a courtyard, where a Mercedes and several other high-end cars were parked. My car looked as out of place as its frumpy-suited driver, and I felt very uncomfortable. I could tell right away that the clients were obviously very wealthy and in a different social strata than me.

As it turned out, my Mercedes-based assumption was correct. They were very wealthy people in their mid-seventies who had been successful in real estate. They were a gracious couple who welcomed me into their home and allowed me to review their life insurance and investments with them. Afterwards, I returned to the office for a follow-up with my manager.

THE QUESTION THAT CHANGED MY PROFESSIONAL AND PERSONAL LIFE FOREVER

Anxious to hear how his new agent had done that evening, my manager asked me, "How did it go?"

I told him about the appointment, what we reviewed, and about how they had become successful selling real estate and building homes.

He then asked, "Did you sell them anything?"

"No," I responded, and I followed it up with a comment that completely surprised my manager. "I can't sell them anything anyway."

Then he asked me the question of questions—the question that would reveal for me the secret to why most people fail in life, fail to realize their dreams, or fail to reach their potential and be successful. It was as much a genius question as it was an indictment against my own twisted thinking and poor self-image as an agent. "Why not?" he asked. "Who told you you can't sell them anything?"

"WHY NOT? WHO TOLD YOU YOU CAN'T SELL THEM ANYTHING?"

He just stood there looking at me with a puzzled expression as a couple seconds ticked by and then walked away. I was embarrassed and somewhat ashamed at the fact that I hadn't thought myself capable of selling this rich, elderly couple one of the products I had to offer.

I did have products and services they could have used, but instead of talking to them about it when I was there for the review, I left without ever broaching the subject, thinking I wasn't worthy or able to sell them anything simply because my suit didn't fit right and my car looked shabby next to theirs.

IF YOU THINK YOU CAN OR YOU THINK YOU CANNOT, YOU ARE RIGHT!

I wish I could end the story of the older couple by telling you I returned for a second appointment after my manager's profound question and sold them something they needed, but that is not what happened.

Yes, I did return in follow-up to suggest some things they might want to consider with their current life insurance program and some other investment options they could pursue with me, but in the end, they didn't buy, and I walked away without making a sale.

Still, sale or no sale, I did walk away with something far more valuable than I could have ever imagined at the time. What I gained was an understanding of the power of self-image to define me, to define my life, to define my outcomes and my success or failures both personally and professionally.

In retrospect, it wasn't my father who told me I couldn't fix things or use my hands for building and repairing things. It wasn't anyone who told me I couldn't fix a garbage disposal or remodel a basement room into an entertainment center. Nor was it any specific person who told me I couldn't sell that older couple anything. It was me who was limiting me!

WHO DEFINES THE REALM OF THE POSSIBLE FOR YOU?

I was the one who was placing limits on my potential and defining boundaries that confined me to being just an academic, or just a mediocre salesman, or just someone who couldn't instead of someone who could do something if he put his mind to it.

How foolish I was! How could I have missed such a lesson? How could I have done this to myself?

HOW ABOUT YOU? WHAT DO YOU THINK ABOUT YOUR ABILITIES & OUR PROFESSION?

Attitude isn't everything; it's the only thing. What do you think about yourself? What do you think about your abilities as an agent, a professional, an expert?

Do you believe you can be successful? Do you think you bring value to people's lives when you consult with them? Do you respect yourself?

BELIEVE IN YOURSELF, AND THE FUTURE IS YOURS

How do you feel about our profession? About being an insurance professional? How do you see yourself in relation to being an insurance agent? Do you feel funny about it, a bit shy, or even a little embarrassed about it because of the public misunderstanding about our industry?

Pull Your Nose Up

Do you think we are noble in our pursuits to sell people insurance and investment products? When people ask you what you do for a living, do you try to avoid telling them the plain truth by masking it in language that paints a picture other than the whole truth?

Have past circumstances somehow convinced you that you can't do something? Have past failures defined for you boundaries that limit your potential to be successful or achieve your dreams? Is your poor self-image telling you you're not good enough for something or not smart enough?

Who is holding you back? Is it you?

Everyone experiences self-doubt, some more than others. We all have some measure of doubt or question whenever we embark on a new endeavor, forge toward a new direction, or undertake a new challenge. Unfamiliarity and uncertainty create a natural tension within each of us. What I am referring to goes deeper and speaks to the core belief you have in yourself, your abilities, and your right to be happy and worthy of success.

WHAT'S HOLDING YOU BACK? WHO IS HOLDING YOU BACK?

> Be sure the boundaries in life that you do encounter are not self-imposed.

You cannot out-perform your own self-image. If you think you can't make those calls, if you think you can't make those sales, if you think you can't achieve that goal, you are right.

Today, if you visit my house, you will see that my garbage disposal works, my basement is finished, and even my garage is dry walled and fitted out like an extra living room in my house. I did all of that because now I know that I am a man of the Earth. Ask me for a tool, and I will get you the right one; I guarantee it. I no longer define myself as an academic. Instead, I am a man who refuses to think he is incapable of doing anything. I am a man who works with his mind and his hands. No longer will I limit myself by poor thinking and a poor self-image.

Am I arrogant for writing such a thing? I don't think so. It is the lesson of self-image—the lesson that says, "You cannot outperform your own self-image"—that allows me to write these words. It is because of the question I was asked years ago: "Why not? Who told you that you can't sell them anything?" I vowed after that experience I was never going to do that to myself again, and I hope you feel the same way.

The Pain of Discipline or the Pain of Regret

"Success is often disguised as hard work." ~ *Unknown*

WHICH DO YOU PREFER?

1. The pain that comes with hard work and waking in the morning to earn a living and be successful…

OR

The pain that comes with the secret knowledge of your own laziness and the underlying causes of your own failure.

2. The pain of practicing and studying to get better at something and to feel the thrill of learning something new…

OR

The pain of never truly mastering anything.

3. The pain of planning and organizing to win or succeed at some noble endeavor…

OR

The pain of always being and feeling overwhelmed, uncertain, and without accomplishment.

4. The pain of accepting and attempting new challenges and experiencing new frontiers and making friendships…

OR

The pain of boredom and emptiness.

5. The pain of setting goals and working toward them, enabling you to own your hard-earned success and the excitement of accomplishment and victory…

OR

The pain of having no direction, no sense of purpose, no fulfillment, and/or no sense of achievement.

6. The pain of cooperation and teamwork and the bond it creates among peers…

OR

The pain of loneliness, rejection, and isolation.

7. The pain of doing right, being honest, and keeping promises as a person of character, integrity, and a good conscience...

OR

The pain of a tarnished reputation, guilt, and a troubled conscience.

The pain of discipline or the pain of regret: which do you prefer for your life?

"Choose well, for your choices are brief, yet eternal." ~ Goethe

E = MC²: A New Theory of Relativity

People are emotionally centered creatures. They crave connection and relationships with other people. Therefore, life is all about relationships. We all have personal and professional relationships. And in every relationship, there are varying degrees of strength or value. Let us look at a new Theory of Relativity, relationship building that everyone should master.

> E = Engagement
> M = Meaningful
> C2 = Conversation between two (2) people

Engagement is true connection and emotional equity. Built through that engagement is meaningful conversations between two people.

Do you want to know the measure of your relationship with a son or daughter, a spouse, or a customer? Then ask yourself this question: "How many meaningful conversations have I had with them? How many in-depth, uninterrupted, full-attention conversations have we had together?" Your answer will be the measure of how strong the bond is between the two of you and how valuable that relationship really is for each party.

How about with your clients? How many conversations have you had with them that touch on their emotional needs? Insurance and financial services professionals, how many one-on-one conversations have you had with clients on topics such as death, college education, dignity and choice in healthcare matters, just to name a few?

It takes time and a lot of personal capital to invest in people this way, but the more $E = MC^2$ tallies you can point to in a relationship, the stronger that relationship is, the more meaningful the relationship, and the more loyal the bond between the two individuals.

$E = MC^2$ is a new theory of relativity, and in business, it can mean the difference between keeping a customer and losing one.

Experience is NOT the Best Teacher

"The world comes to me as a fact, but I decide what to conclude from here." ~ Peter Block, The Answer to How is Yes

What is an experience but the present moment of a particular circumstance? Experiences are as fleeting as they are arresting; as real as they are imagined; and as useful to us as they are benign. They are like the sounds of a pendulum's swing, rushing through the air one moment, while telling the lessons of time about the dial in the next. They are all around us, but alone, experiences they are neither good nor bad, right nor wrong, worthwhile nor a waste—at least not until they are reflected upon and thereby given relevance and meaning.

Thus, contrary to some popular opinion, experience is NOT the best teacher; rather, it is *reflected* experience that is the best instructor of life. Not until something becomes relevant to a person can it ever effect a change in their behavior or thinking. And not until something is reflected upon—a past experience that is pondered, considered, and internalized in search of its meaning and lesson—can it ever become relevant.

RELEVANCE IS DISCERNED THROUGH REFLECTION.
CHANGE IS MADE THROUGH RELEVANCE.

It is at the point of relevance (or realization) that our experiences become useful to us; they change us, and we discover whether the experience was good or bad, right or wrong, worthwhile or a waste. Therefore, reflected experience is the only effective means to get people to change, grow, and be successful.

WHAT DOES ALL THIS MEAN TO THE SALES PROFESSIONAL?

Beware of amassing a lifetime of sales experience that yields no value aside from the commission. Beware of a life that says "Twenty years of sales experience equates to superior sales prowess and success." Whenever the word "experienced" is uttered, it is almost a proverbial truth that it means nothing more than a lot of time accrued in a particular industry. It is sad, but true, that experience counts for nothing in many instances of business conduct. Why? Because sales professionals often never take the time to reflect upon those experiences so they may learn and grow and become a better person and professional as a result.

REFLECTION IS EVALUATION

Evaluate your activities and your sales conversations, and let others do the same. Be honest with yourself when analyzing your marketing efforts and your sales techniques. Formulate a simple method or process (a checklist, for example) that causes you to reflect from time to time on your daily, weekly, monthly, or yearly experiences.

It is not that important how often you reflect upon your experiences as a sales professional, nor is it that important how you evaluate yourself either. What is important is that you do it. Plain and simple as it sounds, you may need to schedule time to reflect upon your business activities and their results. The outcome will be growth for you both personally and professionally.

A FINAL NOTE ON REFLECTED EXPERIENCE

Never expect training to change behavior or to provide a pathway to personal and professional growth. Training—particularly classroom sales training—has no real value in many organizations. Why? Because most training is very brief and impractical and lacks a reflection component. In my current professional capacity, I am extremely fortunate to be a part of an organization that recognizes the need for reflection and evaluation, along with the 'block and tackle' method of training on product and marketing systems and sales techniques. We see much success among the ranks of those agents and leaders we work with and develop, but this is because our situation is unique, and not everyone in sales has access to this type of training or these types of programs. In fact, most organizations fail when it comes to follow-up and reflection, vital pieces of the learning model.

"No one is going to change as a result of our desires." ~ Peter Block, The Answer to How is Yes

Many so-called Learning and Development divisions within sales organizations fail at achieving positive change for sales professionals because follow-up components (reflection and evaluation of sales experience) are oftentimes missing from their training model. These departments would be more accurately named only 'Learning' as opposed to 'Learning and Development' because little to no development ever actually occurs.

Don't be like so many other sales professionals or organizations that never take the time to reflect upon their sales and marketing experiences in order to learn from mistakes and successes.

Experience is NOT the best teacher; it's *reflective* experience that is the best teacher.

The following are examples of some evaluation tools that can be used to reflect upon past behaviors and performance.

Example #1

Tool for Evaluating a Sales Conversation/Appointment

(To be used by the agent or a sales manager following a sales appointment.)

Sales Interview Evaluation Form
(Post-Interview Reflection)

Prospect/Customer Name:_____ Date:_____

Lead Type (current/new contact)

Results: _____ ___   Follow-up/Action Items for
_____   Improvement _____
_____   _____
_____   _____

I. INITIAL CONTACT/OPENING/APPROACH:

	YES	NO		YES	NO
Favorable First Impression			"Thank" them for coming in to meet		
Smile Consciously			Psychological Reciprocity (give-away item, soda)		
Handshake Firm			Any Distractions (exclusive attention given)		
Eye Contact Balanced					
Body Language Attentive (Posture, Gestures)			Establish an Agenda (transition statement)		
Gain Rapport (Emotional Connection) (Family, Occupation, Community Education, Recreation— Get into their World)			Professional attire?		
			Office Environment		

NOTES: (What/How can I improve my opening?) _____
_____
_____

II. THE INTERVIEW:

Dominant Buying Motive/Criteria: _____

	YES	NO		YES	NO
Systematic use of probes (questions)			Did you use trial closes?		
Did you use visuals?			Did you use their names?		
Did you use proof sources?			Did you talk more than them?		

NOTES: (What/How can I improve my interview?) _____
_____
_____

III. THE CLOSE:

	YES	NO		YES	NO
Did you ask for the sale?			Did they trust you?		
Did you close on their dominant buying motive?			Did they like you?		
Did you have a plan for closing?			Did you encounter objections you were unable to overcome?		

What were their/your response? _____
_____
_____

NOTES: (What/How can I improve upon closing?) _____
_____
_____

Example #2

Tool for Evaluating Performance Results & Activities

(Template for an "Accountability" Phone Call or Meeting with an Agent Regarding their Activities & Production Results)

Accountability Call/Meeting

(To be used with Sales manager/Agents/Sales Professionals/ Self-Evaluation)

Opening: Administrative and "housekeeping" issues that need to be communicated.

1. Review of Current Production Results/Targets

    A. Auto: _____

    B. Homeowners': _____

    C. Health: _____

    D. Life: _____

    E. Bank: _____

    F. Commercial: _____

    G. Financial Services: _____

    H. Recruiting/Staffing: _____

        1) How do you feel about your results?

        2) <u>Where</u> do you think you have done well? (Why?)

        3) <u>Where</u> do you think you can improve? (Why?) (How?) (What will it take?)

        4) Review each production goal and result, explain <u>how</u> the results have come about and <u>what</u> you think can be done to improve things in the future.

        5) <u>What</u> are you most pleased about in your production? (Why?) (<u>How</u> will you sustain success?)

6) <u>What</u> are you least pleased about in your production? (Why?) (<u>How</u> to improve?)

7) <u>What</u> specific marketing and sales processes and systems do you have in place? (Need to employ?)

    a.) <u>What</u> is working? (How, Why?)

    b) <u>What</u> plans do you have for the future?

8) <u>What</u> do you need in order to be successful? (<u>How</u> can I help?)

9) <u>What</u> changes, if any, can you make to become more successful?

10) <u>What</u> changes, if any, do you want to see occur in order to help you be successful?

11) <u>What</u> plans do you have for next week to grow in production?

12) <u>What</u> plans do you need to put in place for next week/month/year in order to increase production?

13) <u>What</u> activities must be accomplished in order to hit production goals?

14) <u>What</u> activities must be put in place in order to hit production goals?

Summation/Agreement:

2. Summarize what you have discussed and discovered and gain agreement on those steps/processes that will be worked on, production targets that are being aimed at, activities that must be put in motion, and goals that must be met.

A. Item #1: _____
_____
_____

B. Item #2: _____
_____
_____

C. Item #3: _____
_____
_____

What have we decided upon as your next action(s)?

What are the expected outcomes?

What will be the measure of success/accomplishment?

When will we next meet/call to review your actions and results?

Meeting/Call Notes: _____
_____
_____
_____
_____

Example #3

Tool for Evaluating Weekly Marketing and Sales Activities

Weekly Activity Checkup

Name: _____ Date: _____

I. MARKETING ACTIVITIES:

	Appointments Set	Appointments Kept
A. Appointments from "Calling Out" systems		
B. Appointments from "Call-In/Walk-in" Pivot Systems		
C. Appointments from referral systems		
D. Appointments from "introductions" (outside marketing, seminars, networking, centers-of-influence, other)		
	TOTAL SET:	TOTAL KEPT:

1. <u>How</u> many contacts did I make in order to set sales appointments for the week?

2. <u>What</u> was my "call out" activity? (Dials, lead type: "warm/cold")

3. <u>How</u> can I improve my sales appointment setting results? (word track, voice)

4. <u>Where</u> can I use help/assistance with setting sales appointments?

5. <u>What</u> preparations do I make to call out, pivot, secure referrals, other?

6. <u>Where</u> can I improve my sales appointment setting skills/results?

7. <u>What</u> "other" activities can I do in order to set sales appointments?

8. <u>What</u> are my goals? (appointments)

E. Direct Mail Activities

1. What current campaigns (sequential marketing) internally (in-book) and externally do I have actively going?

2. What results am I getting from these marketing campaigns?

3. How might I improve on the appointment/sales results from these marketing campaigns?

4. What other marketing campaigns might we use in order to increase production?

5. What plans do you have for future marketing campaigns?

6. Where are we in relation to the established marketing plan for the year?

7. What is our status on the marketing/budgeting expenditures?

Weekly Activity Checkup
(continued)

Name: _____ Date:_____

II. SALES ACTIVITIES

A. Number of appointments/sales conversations	
B. Number of Sales Closed (total)	
C. Weekly Sales Goal	

1. What is my closing ratio to sales appointment?

2. How can I improve upon my closing ratio?

3. What can I do to speak to more prospects and close more sales?

4. Where might I improve—in my marketing activities or my sales conversation? (Why and How)

5. What are my sales goals? Results?

NOTES: _____
_____
_____
_____
_____

Successful People Know Their Numbers

"Know the score—it's hard to win if you don't know the score, so it's essential to constantly track and measure your sales and the numbers behind the sales." ~ Jack Mitchell, Hug Your Customers

When I was first a salesman in Youngstown, Ohio, I had a wonderful sales manager and sales coach by the name of Chuck who guided my career in the right direction at the onset. He was a true craftsman of the sales profession and a practitioner of the disciplines it took to be successful.

I remember once growing impatient with Chuck when he insisted we spend some time together to discuss and understand my production benchmarks and how my bonuses and pay were stipulated in my contract. Back then, all I cared about was sell, sell, sell.

So I said to Chuck, "Why don't we just skip all the boring paperwork stuff and the training on how I get paid and instead get to something really meaningful like sales techniques and marketing ideas? Besides, I figure if I sell more, I make more, right?"

IF I SELL MORE, I MAKE MORE, RIGHT?

Chuck never relented to my ranting and always insisted that I understood and knew what my auto, homeowners', life, health, mutual funds, and annuity sales benchmarks were. He also always insisted on reviewing my pay scale periodically, as well as the bonuses I was eligible to earn.

He didn't stop there either. Periodically, he would see me in the office and ask, "Hey, where are you with life applications and premiums for your next bonus?"

The first time he asked me that, I replied, "I'm not sure. Let me check, and I'll get back with you."

His response was, "That's unacceptable. You should know them off the top of your head."

"Why?" I said. "I'll have them for you in a minute… just give me a second."

It was at that moment that Chuck taught me one of the most valuable lessons I could learn outside of any sales training class or marketing seminar I could attend. "You'll never be successful with that kind of thinking," he scolded. "Successful people know their numbers, Tony. Remember that! How can you hit something when you can't see it? Hitting the target means knowing where to aim. It sounds to me like you don't know where you're going. Am I right?"

KNOWING YOUR NUMBERS PROVIDES YOU WITH A LINE OF SIGHT TOWARD SUCCESS

He was right, and the lesson was clear. If I ignored what was required of me by the company—or if I ignored the possibilities of achieving sales bonuses and recognition levels—how could I ever achieve success?

Pull Your Nose Up

In the years following that fateful discussion with Chuck, I have had the advantage of observing the differences between successful sales professionals and unsuccessful sales professionals through the eyes of my former mentor and manager. One of the common threads that have separated the two groups from each other is the constant ability of the successful ones to be able to recite their production numbers whenever asked, right off the top of their heads.

What does tracking your numbers mean to you, the sales professional? Better yet, what does knowing your numbers say of you as a sales professional?

Knowing your numbers means you are goal and achievement oriented in a concrete way. It means that, at the end of the day, success is a practical matter for the agency; success is a number that can be pointed to, graphed, counted, measured, and understood in a meaningful and understandable way by everyone.

1. Knowing your numbers means <u>you appreciate and value quantifiable results</u>, as well as the non-quantifiable benefits of being an agent—like the intangible benefits of a better quality of life or more liberty to control your own work schedule. Knowing your numbers means you are a goal-oriented individual, and that is a good thing to be if you want to be successful.

2. Knowing your numbers means <u>you are competitive in nature and driven to succeed</u>. If you know your numbers, you are the kind of person who keeps track of things for a reason, and those reasons are often connected to a competitive nature.

3. Knowing your numbers means <u>you strive to be a winner</u>. Track your numbers to win that bonus that incentive trip, that personal goal you've established for yourself, or that challenge placed before you by the company or sales leaders. Knowing your numbers says you are not only driven by goals, but also by competition. It indicates a spirit of excellence which sparks us to be better than someone else or even our own selves. Winning—like being goal

oriented—is a good thing too. I prefer it over the alternative of losing any day.

4. Knowing your numbers means <u>you understand that "what gets measured gets done."</u> Tracking and knowing your numbers places a focus and attention on specific activities that produce tangible results. That focus and attention translates into a heightened awareness toward execution and the implementation of activities that are meaningful and worthwhile.

5. Knowing your numbers means <u>you understand the power of accountability and how an awareness of the numbers helps you stay focused</u> on activities that yield results. Results are what being a sales professional is all about.

6. Knowing your numbers means <u>you like a thrill and relish challenges as opportunities to shine.</u> Thrills can inject passion and energy into any endeavor in life.

Today, this very moment, regardless of the sales industry you work in, what are your numbers? What are your benchmarks for success, for achievement, and for higher income and benefits? Where are you right now in relation to your numbers? Do you know the answer to any of these questions?

Your future career and success as a sales professional hinges on whether or not you know your numbers!

Psychological Reciprocity

There is a concept in sales called *psychological reciprocity* which, when employed effectively, can help an agent improve their overall closing ratio. Simply said, psychological reciprocity can be described as a feeling of indebtedness by one person when another person gives them something of value.

It is a naturally occurring psychological phenomenon that we have all applied at one time or another whether consciously or not. In its most basic form, psychological reciprocity is evidenced by an offer for a cup of coffee or a small promotional give-away item such as a keychain that advertises your business.

When employed in a sales environment, a prospect will feel obligated and compelled to give something back. At a minimum, that 'return gift' takes the form of a willingness to be candid, open in their responses to questions, and willing to engage in an in-depth sales conversation. At best, the principle of psychological reciprocity can result in the 'gift' of a sale to the agent.

If you want to take advantage of psychological reciprocity, take a look at the marketing materials and promotional pieces you use to attract customers to your storefront or website, etc. Keep those at your desk, pre-positioned, ready to give to your customers as part of the interview routine.

A nice giveaway piece might be a business calendar with your branding on it. What you give is not as important as the fact that you give something, as it really is the thought that counts when it comes to creating a sense of indebtedness. Your sale could be dependent on something as simple as offering refreshment (coffee, soda, or a bottle of water). Even small giveaway promotional pieces (pens, for instance) that many agents have available to them, no matter how simple and inexpensive they may be, are effective in triggering this important human reaction.

Customers do respond positively to our generosity and good-natured message behind the gift. Never, ever, ever underestimate the power of generosity… and never, ever, ever be without a gift, an item, or an offer of something to each customer, particularly when you first meet them. Failing to be prepared with a giveaway item for your customers will result in missing out on an opportunity to differentiate yourself from your competition.

To Make Them Thirsty, Make the Well Run Dry

There's an old English proverb that goes like this: "You never know the worth of water until the well is dry." In other words, the 'value' of something has everything to do with 'need'.

The title of my first book, *Sales Is a Contact Sport*, explained the emotional mental process that customers go through in arriving at the decision to buy or not to buy a particular product or service. I used the word *contact* in the title to emphasize that sales professionals must be cognizant of the need to make emotional contact or connection with people in order to sell more effectively.

If sales is a contact sport and people are emotionally centered and logically dispersed in nature, then it behooves us as sales professionals to make emotional contact with customers—to get emotional with them and strike at the core of what moves them to want to buy.

For insurance and financial services professionals, I suggest you consider the following as a means of achieving emotional connection:

WRECK 'EM (auto insurance)
BURN 'EM (homeowners insurance)
KILL 'EM (life insurance)

Anthony D. Cefalu

MAKE 'EM SICK (health insurance)

At first glance, what I have written appears cold and irresponsible, but what I am suggesting is that sales professionals must resist the urge to tiptoe around the hard issues of life that face us all. We should have the courage to initiate the difficult conversations of life in order to make sure our customers are fully protected and prepared as much as possible for the tragedies of life that can befall anyone. And, even more importantly, it is our professional and our moral obligation to warn people of the risks they are exposing themselves to…and how to plan against their affects.

For example, when broaching the difficult subject of life insurance, the tendency of insurance agents is to illustrate a scenario about some fictitious third party person—some hypothetical situation in which an unnamed husband or wife dies and leaves the family penniless. Such an approach that is taken by an agent is an attempt to avoid the accusation of being dark, insensitive and fear mongering. Therefore, rather than illustrate a scenario involving the customer being spoken to, the agent attempts to soften the shocking possibility of tragedy by speaking in a third party fashion. That is a mistake.

Instead, be direct with the people who are sitting across the table from you. Make them the tragic victim in an illustration. Help them to understand the realities of what can happen to them in the event of the death of a loved one. Ask them how their family will cope financially as a result. Use their names to paint the picture of what could and will be if they die without adequate protection. That is emotion—that is what I call, *contact*. Making a real, human connection with a customer on a personal and emotional level is what agents need to do to sell well while simultaneously serving their customers' needs.

For example:

"Tom, if you were to die today, how would Mary and your daughter Lisa and son Mike be able to maintain the lifestyle you two have built for yourselves? What would happen to this home? To their college education? How will Mary take care of all those things without you? How will she pay the mortgage? Where would the lost income come from to provide for the basic needs of your children, Lisa and Mike?"

OR

"Tom, if you were to be the at-fault driver in a serious automobile accident while on vacation and you, Mary, and the kids were hurt—for example, if you had a broken arm—what would you do about the medical bills that followed, especially if you couldn't work to pay for them? Rather than hassle with worrying about whether being in-network or out-of-network with your healthcare provider from work, wouldn't it be worth it to have the peace of mind to know that adequate medical payments coverage was part of your auto policy? That way, your family could avoid the worry and potential of out-of-pocket expenses that always follow an accident and instead can focus on the important things, like you getting better."

OR

"Tom, what would happen today if you and Mary were to have a house fire, leaving you with a total loss, only to discover that your coverage is inadequate to fully rebuild this beautiful house? Where would you live? How would little Lisa and Mike cope with losing all their things and having to live somewhere different and strange without the prospect of ever returning to the home they are familiar with and secure in? Would you have to move in with relatives until it was all sorted out—months or maybe even years down the road? Would that really be convenient for you? Would it be an unnecessary burden on them?"

OR

"Tom, if you were to require nursing home care—say, as a result of a stroke—how would you and Mary cope with the added expense of your care? How would you be able to afford it? Where would the money come from to pay for your care? What would you do, in the meantime, for grocery money, utilities, all those expenses we incur just to survive and live on a daily basis? Could your family continue the lifestyle they have today? What effect would that have on the family?"

The proverb is true: People never know the worth of water until the well has run dry. Do your customers a favor (and yourself, for that matter) and have the courage to be direct with people when talking to them about the risks of inadequate insurance protection. When you talk to them, make the well run dry so that they will be prepared and won't die of thirst when the time really does come! We owe it to them to:

WRECK 'EM
BURN 'EM
KILL 'EM
MAKE 'EM SICK

… your customers will thank you for it.

Brief Is Better

In 1863, Abraham Lincoln delivered one of history's most famous and remembered speeches, "The Gettysburg Address." It was 273 words and took only two minutes to deliver. The main address that day, which preceded Lincoln's famous one, was given by Harvard president and statesman, Edward Everett. He was considered to be one of the greatest orators of his time. Everett's speech lasted two hours.

Of the two, which speech is the most memorable or talked about by historians? "The Gettysburg Address," of course. It is remembered and revered and weaved into the very fabric of our nation's history.

Things are no different in the present day than they were for good ol' Abe. How long was your last sales presentation? Did you consciously and strategically present a powerful and persuasive sales conversation? Or, did you give in to the urge of telling the prospect everything you know about auto or life insurance, rambling on and on, even just a little?

BREVITY IS THE SOUL OF WIT AND WISDOM

What does *brevity* mean for the insurance and financial services sales expert? It means you should keep your sales presentations on point, direct, well thought out, and planned (scripted).

Anthony D. Cefalu

LISTEN PEOPLE INTO BUYING

Talk less. Not only will a concise, purposeful sales presentation positively affect the enthusiasm of those listening to you, but it can also impact your own morale during the effort. If you've ever had the unfortunate experience of someone glancing at their watch or yawning while you were giving your presentation, you know all too well the negative psychological impact a bored prospect can have on the momentum of a sales conversation.

Invest some time in deliberately pruning your sales presentations of unneeded discussion points and statements. For every point and every line you script out ask yourself, "Why is this needed for my presentation?" If you're not sure of the reason, cut it out of the script. Lean and effective is your goal.

Remember to have a game plan when it comes to your sales presentations. Think of it as a road map to effective communication and persuasion. Plans allow for flexibility and the liberty to deviate as the situation dictates. Without a plan, you've got nothing to deviate from or be flexible with when talking to prospects.

Stupid Things I've Heard & What I Think When I Hear Them

Take inventory of your language and avoid phrases that might make listeners (customers) defensive or make you sound uncertain, lacking in confidence, weak, stupid, and even a bit manipulative in some instances.

Here are some of the mistakes I hear sales professionals make over the phone and in face-to-face sales conversations, along with what I think when I hear them:

What I've Heard: "I guess I'll let you get back to your work."

What I Think: "Quit guessing. I've already gone back."

What I've Heard: "I don't want to take anymore of your time."

What I Think: "Then don't, you little thief!"

What I've Heard: "I'm sure it's time for you to get back to business."

What I Think: "You are sooo perceptive!"

Anthony D. Cefalu

What I've Heard: "I hope this is what you are looking for."
What I Think: "Hope is a good thing."

What I've Heard: "Would it be convenient for you if I took a few moments of your time?"
What I Think: "Nope. I only have so many heartbeats allocated to me in this lifetime."

What I've Heard: "I just wanted to give you a call today to see if you'd be interested in…"
What I Think: "That's nice to know, but no thanks."

What I've Heard: "I was recently assigned your file, and…"
What I Think: "Now that makes me feel special. So, I'm just a file to you?"

What I've Heard: "If I could show you how you could save money, you'd want to hear more, wouldn't you?"
What I Think: "Just back me into a corner, why don't you?"

What I've Heard: "Could I have a few moments of your time?"
What I Think: "Nope!"

What I've Heard: "Sorry to bother you, but…"
What I Think: "Apology accepted. Goodbye!"

What I've Heard: "Is this a bad time?"
What I Think: "Now that you mention it, yes it is!"

Pull Your Nose Up

What I've Heard: "I was wondering if you might be interested in..."

What I Think: "Well, you can stop wondering. I'm not."

Other weak phrases and words to avoid include:
- "Sort of."
- "Kind of."
- "This is probably the answer." (or worse yet, "...prolly the answer."
- "It should help" or "I think this should help."
- "I can't/won't/don't do that."

These wishy-washy words and phrases fail to engender confidence between you and the customer.

As a sales expert, advisor, and advocate for your customers, you should never find yourself saying "can't, won't, or don't" to a customer. Try "I'm not able to..." instead, as it is a better way of saying things.

Also stay away from phrases like, "To be perfectly honest..." or "To tell you the truth..." to which the customer might mentally respond, "What? You mean you haven't been perfectly honest with me or told me the truth until now?"

Additionally, "You know," "pretty much," and "whatnot" are overused phrases that serve only to weaken your language and the perception the customer may have of you ever being a competent, capable insurance agent. These phrases are momentum killers in the sales conversation, so make it a point to drop them from your language altogether.

Anthony D. Cefalu

Use positive mental words such as:

You	Happy	Value
We	Satisfied	Smart
Us	Enjoy	Determine
Together	Productive	Choice
Work through	Answer	Variety
Thanks	Idea	Brilliant
Great	Improve	Excellent
Wonderful	Fix	Powerful
Terrific	Relieve	
I'm glad	Discuss	

Words like these have energy and conjure positive images in the mind of the listener.

Don't be guilty of these common violations of the English language:

- "Irregardless" is not a proper word. Say "regardless" instead.
- It's not a "mute point"; it is a "moot point."
- Avoid saying "ba bye." Instead, try saying "Goodbye" or "Thank you. Have a nice day."
- Equally unprofessional is "okie dokie."

Practicing the use of good English with customers makes you appear more knowledgeable and professional, and we all want that, don't we?

The Difference

Growing up, I loved watching Jack Nicklaus golfing on TV with such greats as Lee Trevino, Arnold Palmer, Tom Watson, Gary Player, and Tom Weiskopf, just to name a few. He was great to watch. My father idolized him and considered him the greatest golfer that ever lived. These days, Tiger Woods, his current list of titles notwithstanding, still has some work to do in order to assume the crown from Nicklaus.

At his peak during the PGA tour, Jack Nicklaus reportedly earned approximately $400,000, an extraordinary amount of winnings in any era, especially in the 1960s.

There was another golfer, a contemporary of Nicklaus's, by the name of Bob Charles. Although a good golfer by anyone's standard (good enough to have achieved professional status and a place on the PGA tour), Charles was not as successful as Nicklaus. In fact, during that same time, Charles made only about one-tenth of what Nicklaus earned, about $40,000 on the same tour. There was certainly a huge difference in income, but there was also an amazing contrast between the two professional golfers.

Even more incredible than the difference in their respective incomes was the difference between their levels of play, their performance on the green. Jack Nicklaus's actual performance per round was less than half-a-stroke better on average than that of Bob Charles's. Wow! The difference between the greatest golfer of all time and his high income and a very good golfer without nearly the income was less than a half-stroke per round! It was such a large difference in outcome when compared to the small difference in their performance.

What does this tell us about ourselves, our profession, and the noble pursuit we, as insurance agents and financial services providers, work toward every day? Better asked, what *should* it tell us about ourselves, our profession, the pursuit of excellence, and the honor of being the greatest professional we can be? Oftentimes, the difference between good and great is a very small thing: an extra call to a customer about life insurance, a handwritten note to comfort someone who was in an automobile accident, or setting another appointment to achieve your production goal for the month.

Whatever that little extra thing is, just do it. Up your game just one half-stroke more each day so you can get the advantage over the competition that you deserve—so you can be happier and enjoy an income that your rivals will envy.

It really is the little things we do that make the biggest difference in our lives and in the lives of our insureds. It's the difference that makes us different!

It Does Matter Who You Know

Frustrated and unsuccessful salespeople often say, "It is not fair. What you know doesn't matter. It's who you know that does."

The question I have for individuals who make such claims is: What's so unfair about that? Now, I believe there is a need for knowing and being professional and competent, but what is so wrong with knowing the 'right people', so to speak, and capitalizing on those relationships to accomplish your goals?

It sounds more like resentment to me rather than an issue of fairness when I hear the complaints of those who criticize the value of relationships in such a manner. Life is about relationships, and business is woven in the fabric of our everyday lives. What is true about everyday life is equally true about business; it is all about relationships.

For the moment, let us imagine I am as equally repulsed as other individuals by the statement, "What you know doesn't matter as much as who you know, especially when it comes to job opportunities, career advancement, and personal or professional success."

What gain is there in refusing to accept the fact that relationships and the power they have in influencing people and achieving success in life over knowledge, subject matter expertise, or experience? The answer is that nothing is gained when that attitude is adopted.

Anthony D. Cefalu

To deny the role that relationships play in creating opportunity for success in business and in life is to deny an immutable reality of human nature.

Why not use your network of relationships to gain access to people in order to sell the greatest product to have ever been conceived by the mind of man? Frankly, that's how a lot of business and commerce works: by way of relationships.

IF YOU WANT TO BE SUCCESSFUL IN LIFE, YOU MUST UNDERSTAND HOW LIFE WORKS

In order to be successful in life, you must find ways to work with or around life and its challenges, opportunities, and setbacks.

Set aside the issue of fairness when people leverage their relationships to get what they want in business. Just acknowledge the fact that it does matter who you know and go on with your life. Begin to embrace the realities of how life works and build your circle of influential and helpful relationships. There's nothing wrong with leveraging friendships and acquaintances. People helping other people are what make commerce—and life—work.

GAIN ACCESS TO PEOPLE THROUGH PEOPLE

Networking—no matter how unpalatable it may be to the high minded—is a fact of life and a legitimate means of gaining access to people who need your expertise.

People need you and what you have to offer. What better justification is there for leveraging relationships to your advantage than the fact that the general public needs your expertise as an insurance and financial services professional? How unfair or distasteful can it be for you, then, to network among your acquaintances to gain access to other people, set appointments under favorable conditions, and avoid the normal resistance encountered with truly cold contacts?

Consider the Following:

Have a game plan—an opening statement you are comfortable with in meeting new people. In some instances, being prepared to share who you are and what you do for people is an excellent pattern to follow when making introductions with new acquaintances. Some call this their 'elevator speech' or their 'thirty-second commercial'.

The following are some possible ways to introduce yourself to individuals and to begin building your network of influence, friends, and helpful relationships.

> *"Hi, I'm Tom Smith. This is my first meeting here. Are you a member?"*

(Get people talking about themselves and what they feel is important. Be interested in people. Find out what they do for an occupation, where they were born, and what hobbies they may be involved in. Also, ask about family, kids, and names; these are all things that will help with building rapport and connection with the people you meet.)

OR

> *"Hi, I'm Tom Smith. I'm new to the group. How about you? Are you a member? Have you been attending long?"*

OR

> *"Hi, I'm Tom Smith. I was wondering if you could help me with something. This is my first meeting, and I really don't know anyone. Would it be possible for you to introduce me to some of your members?"*

The following is a word track that can possibly be used in a setting where you are addressing the host/hostess of a meeting or a center of influence in a business gathering:

> *"Hi, I'm Tom Smith, an insurance agent with XYZ Company here in the Atlanta area. I work with business owners just like you in helping them use their insurance dollars as best as they can while helping them to improve their bottom line results. Oftentimes, I'm able to help reduce a business owners expenses while at the same time ensuring they are completely protected... and that's important in our "sue happy" society."*

Whatever the approach, make sure it is one you are comfortable with delivering and owning. Think about using the phraseology, "Could you help me?" These are powerful words to use with people.

One of the greatest of human desires is the desire to be wanted and to be a help to people. Strangers naturally respond positively to such requests for help.

Pull Your Nose Up

> *"I wonder if you could help me. I've wanted to meet Frank Stone now for weeks and haven't had the opportunity or occasion to talk to him. I understand you two know each other, and I was wondering if you could help me by introducing me to him."*

Having friends, building relationships with people, and enlarging your universe of personal and business acquaintances will not only enrich your life personally, but it has practical utility as well when it comes to enriching your professional and business endeavors.

Make friends and use them. By that statement, I don't mean an individual should be selfishly mercenary and have friends for the sole purpose of getting something out of them. On the contrary, what I am suggesting is that sales professionals utilize the resources available to them through their relationships in order to gain access to people that can use their services and expertise because, in the end, it does matter who you know.

The Whole Package

In the auto and homeowners' insurance sales arena, I often hear sales professionals declare grudgingly, "It's all about price these days. I don't care what anyone says. Price rules."

I understand why they say such things, especially when a competitor's premium comes in $100 less a half (six-month premium) than their stated premium. Situations like this are very frustrating to the insurance professional.

As a result, the conversation ends, the white flag of surrender is raised, and the salesperson politely smiles, wishing the prospective customer Godspeed while secretly hoping a year from now, the tables will be turned on the competition when they have to raise their rates above theirs.

This is not the attitude or the approach any professional advisor in insurance matters should adopt. I do realize that scenarios like the one just mentioned are played out every day in the life of an insurance professional. People are concerned with the cost of things, but I also realize people don't base their buying decisions solely on the weight of price.

People are looking for value, and value is simply the relationship between price and the benefits of having a product or service. Value is something that is different from person to person. It is a highly personal, subjective matter. Therefore, our challenge as sales professionals is to uncover what it is a particular person values or deems personally important to them. Until then, a persuasive sales conversation cannot occur.

SELLING IS A TRANSACTION OF VALUE

Sales is a contact sport, but I would add that *sales is a transaction of value* as well. People are emotional creatures who desire to be wanted, to feel special, and to associate and buy from people they perceive to be like them. As emotional creatures, we base our decisions to act and to buy on emotion first and then we later justify our emotional impulses to buy with logic. It is part of our natural 'wiring' as human beings to process our thinking and to take action in that order.

Bringing it back to the realm of auto and homeowners' insurance sales, people will look at the price but will buy based on the emotional benefits they perceive will result from buying from you, your company, and your agency.

BENEFIT SELLING IS VALUE SELLING

Think about when you purchase things, particularly things of a significant nature and of great value to you. Ask yourself the following, "What is it that causes me to buy from one place or vendor versus another?" In other words, what is the reason why you buy a particular thing from a particular person at a particular place, especially when you have choices to go with someone else or go some other place to buy?

Without exception, the list of responses I receive to these questions is dominated with comments such as:
- "The salesperson was friendly and/or knowledgeable."
- "It was a nice environment"
- "They weren't pushy, and I wasn't pressured."
- "I felt they care about me and my needs."
- "I buy from people I trust."

- "I didn't feel stupid when I asked questions,"
- "They made me feel special."
- "They let me decide."
- "I felt comfortable."
- "They took their time with me."
- "They responded quickly to my questions."

Absent from the list of responses is the issue of price. That is not because price fails to be an issue. No, the reason it is not found on the list is because it fails to be 'high' on the list of reasons why people buy. Price does eventually get mentioned as a factor in why people buy, it just is not THE factor, or high priority factor that drives the decision within people to buy something or to not buy something. Other elements are more important to consumers.

Independent research with investors/buyers lists the top six priorities people value when choosing to work with financial advisors as:
1. Understand my situation.
2. Educate me.
3. Respect my assets.
4. Solve my problems.
5. Monitor my progress.
6. Keep in touch.

Price is not commonly found as a top priority when people decide to buy.

PRICE DOES MATTER, BUT IT ISN'T THE WHOLE MATTER

It's not that price isn't an issue for people, because it does matter. But price is not necessarily the whole issue for people when it comes to choosing to buy one thing over another or one place over another to transact business. Emotions rule, and relationships matter. It's at the origin of feelings and emotion that people link the price to value and worth. It's how people decide... to decide.

So, to those who declare, "It's all about price these days," consumer behavior and industry research historically validates that it is more than just price that primarily drives the buying impulse for individuals. Price does matter; please do not misunderstand me on that point. An insurance company's pricing structure has to make sense and be market competitive in order for agents to be able to sell. However, understand when I say that the evidence and my observations on human behavior during the buying process confirm that price is not the whole matter. In fact, it is not even in the top three in regard to researched reasons why people buy or choose not to buy.

You may be asking, "So now what? What am I to do with this information? What does this all mean for me as an insurance sales expert, an agent?" Well, what it means is that we have to begin looking at our products, particularly auto and homeowners insurance, less as a commodity sale based on price and more on the emotional aspect of the sales spectrum.

It means we have to begin selling the whole package when it comes to the art of the sale. We have to look at things differently—to begin communicating the emotional benefits of the whole package to the customer so they can make the favorable value connection between price and the benefits of owning our auto and homeowners' insurance products. Simply put, we need to get prospective customers to see that the premium is worth all that we say it is worth.

How do you do that? How do you get people to realize that your price is worth it? You do this by helping them discover all those things about you, your company, and your agency that make you so valuable and unique to them in comparison to the competition. You create value and emotional connection with people by telling them your story and by telling them what is in it for them if they choose to buy from you. Being a sales professional is about selling the whole package…selling the benefits of buying…selling the value

THE VALUE DIAMOND CONCEPT

What exactly is *the whole package*? Well, the whole package deals with leveraging and linking what we understand about the emotional buying nature of people to the value proposition of four interrelated factors: (1) Price, (2) Product, (3) the Person selling, and (4) the Place where people buy. I call this relationship the *Value Diamond Concept*.

Similar to what is taught and depicted to help firefighters understand the relationship of the key elements to creating a fire, the Value Diamond Concept demonstrates how the various elements of Price, Product, the Person, and the Place all work together to create a sense of value for the customer.

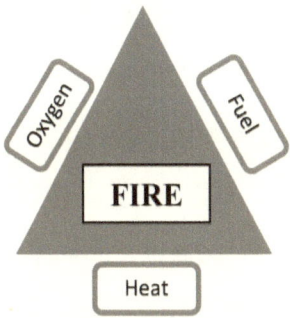

Take away any key element in the 'fire triangle' (as depicted above), and fire cannot exist or is greatly diminished. The same holds true for value. Remove or diminish one of the four key elements of value, and you remove value altogether or diminish the persuasive impact of a sales conversation.

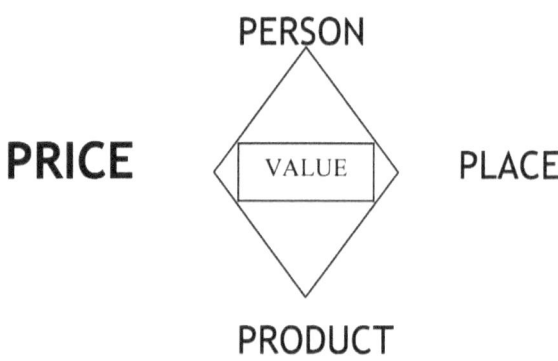

Graphically, that is what the whole package looks like. All four factors are dependent upon each other, working to make the decision to buy from you, the agent, worth it. Let's examine each of these factors briefly and see how they affect the overall motive of the customer to buy.

1) THE PRICE FACTOR

Price Does Not Have Meaning or Relevance until it Is Compared to Something

Price is the quantitative measure of what someone must pay in order to get something. It is sterile, clinical, precise, and rational, and, as such, registers on the left side of the brain—that part of our anatomy which analyzes and computes but does not make the overriding decisions in our lives, including the decision to buy.

Price Is a Measure, Much Like Fahrenheit or Centigrade

Price is what it is: a number and nothing more. You can't change it. When presented to a customer, apart from all other factors, it has no meaning. Just as Centigrade and Fahrenheit have no meaning without relevance to something that is understood or known. For example, zero degrees Fahrenheit is neither hot or cold to one's understanding unless it is realized by the individual to be cold by either experiencing zero degrees Fahrenheit personally or being taught that it is cold by temperature standards. Without relevance, or comparison to something known or understood, the price of something cannot be defined as 'bad' or 'good'. Thus, when discussing price, juxtaposition is crucial to persuading people to buy.

In those instances where the price presented to a prospect is higher than the competitor price the individual is currently paying, changing companies is defined as 'bad'. When the new price is lower than the current competitor's price, changing companies is defined by the individual as 'good'.

Sadly and far too often, that is how selling is approached particularly in light of how auto and homeowners insurance is concerned.

OUR GREAT FOLLY AS SALES PROFESSIONALS

Our great folly as insurance professionals is to allow the customer to define the rules of relevance. Instead, when it comes to the price of our product, we should shift the customer's thinking and focus from what they are currently paying in auto insurance to what they can potentially *get* from us as a result of the price we have shared with them. This is powerful in terms of combating a competitor's lower price. Many agents make the mistake of failing to tell the customer what it is they are getting for the price they are asking.

Perspective is just as important for the agent as it is for the customer. If agents would be more effective at articulating the benefits of what a customer is getting and approach the sales conversation from that angle, that perspective, customers would buy more often even when they can get a lower price offer elsewhere.

Anthony D. Cefalu

THE ONLY WAY TO COMBAT A COMPETITOR'S LOWER PRICE IS TO COMMUNICATE HIGHER VALUE

A better way of communicating price is to shift the customer's thinking away from looking solely at what they are paying now and provoking their thought processes to consider the benefits of what they will get when buying from you.

SHIFT CUSTOMER THINKING TO AN ALTERNATIVE STANDARD OF RELEVANCE

For example:

"The premium for the first six months, Tom, is $500. That's just a little more than $80 a month, under $3.00 (about $2.75) a day. For less than the price of a daily cup of coffee, you can make sure that you, Peggy, and the girls are properly protected if they are ever in an accident.

"Peggy, for you, driving all the way to Columbus, a forty-mile one-way commute every morning and evening is grueling—not to mention dangerous. A lot of accidents do happen on the beltway around the city. This plan is structured to give you the peace of mind knowing that if you are ever in an accident going to work, you are protected for any potential damage to your car and the other person's car, as well as any injuries that anyone sustains.

"And correct me if I'm wrong, Tom, but one of the things you mentioned at the beginning of our discussion was how frustrated you were with your last agent because he wouldn't return your phone calls and didn't seem to care if you needed anything. I know that must have been very frustrating. Please keep this in mind when considering an insurance agent, as 1,600 other families just like yours choose us and trust us to take care of their insurance needs. If you are to choose us as your insurance carrier today, I promise you we will treat you like family as well. We'll be there for you when you need help or have a question or concern about your family's protection needs.

"In fact, here is my business card. My toll-free number is right there, Tom, and here's one for Peggy as well. You can reach a live person 24/7 at that number. And if ever you call and we don't have the answer for you right then—which is rare with all the experience we have here in the office—we'll find the answer for you and get back with you. We have a policy of getting back with our insured within twenty-four hours, often much sooner. We do this so our customers know we are working for them, doing the worrying for them so they don't have to, and that we care about them and appreciate their business. That's just how we work here at the Broad Street Insurance Agency. How does that sound, Tom? Peggy? Great."

I am not suggesting that as a sales professional, I can get a customer to forget about the premium they are currently paying, especially if it is significantly lower than what has just been quoted to them by you. That would not be a realistic expectation.

What is realistic and possible is for the agent to get the customer to shift their perspective and focus away from the difference in price and to get them to consider what it is they _get_ for the price just quoted versus what they have to _give_ up to go with you. This is a subtle difference in the sales conversation, but an extremely powerful difference, nonetheless, in the resultant outcome for an agent to close a sale.

FROM A CUSTOMER PERSPECTIVE, GETTING IS BETTER THAN GIVING

Instead of the customer silently thinking, "The premium is $500 every six months, but I pay $400 now. I'd have to _give_ up $100 to go with Broad Street Insurance as my agent," influence their thinking in the direction of value and the good things they get from buying from you. Do this, and the customer's mental processing will be more along the lines of, "So that's what I _get_ for $100 if I go with Broad Street as my agent? That's a better buy for my money."

Anthony D. Cefalu

Does Shifting the Customer's Mental Energy Away from Their Current Company Work All the Time?

Does this technique work every time it is used? Of course not, but then again, I subscribe to hockey legend Wayne Gretsky's philosophy: "You miss 100 percent of the shots you don't take." So take the shot! Eventually, you'll be scoring points on cases you never thought you had a chance to win.

Don't be one dimensional as a sales professional, always relying on price to make the sale, hoping your premium is less than the competitions. That's no way to live or prosper as an insurance agent. It reduces our profession to no more than 'order takers' and makes us no different from what the Internet has to offer.

2) THE PRODUCT FACTOR

Product, in terms of an influential factor of value, is equally as benign as price when it stands apart from all other factors. In some instances, a competing company's product will have more features and benefits than yours, while in other instances; your product will have more features and benefits than theirs.

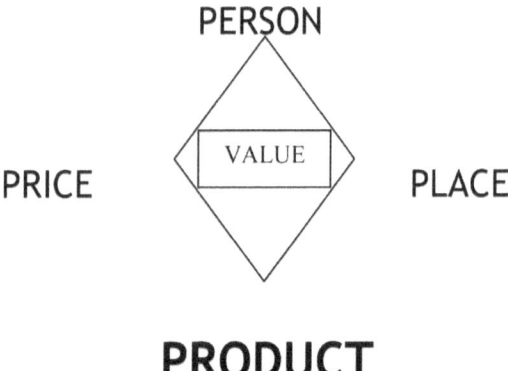

Like price, product is quantitative, factual, and sterile in nature. It is what it is—nothing more and nothing less. So when we sell on product features, we tend to close only on those sales where our product is clearly superior to the competition. We fail to close on those sales where we do not excel in features by comparison.

PRICE & PRODUCT ARE LEFT-BRAIN FACTORS IN THE VALUE DIAMOND

I am not discounting the impact that price and product have on a customer's buying decision. They are important factors in a person's perception of value. By their very nature, price and product are left-brain-functioning elements of any value proposition. They are factually based elements that are points of discussion in a sales conversation and are predominantly processed in the left brain, a physical place in our minds that is naturally dispassionate, calculating, and unemotional.

For example, when discussing product with a customer a stronger and more compelling alternative, right-brain way to communicate may sound like this:

"Included in your auto insurance plan is rental car coverage. If ever you are in an accident and your car requires repairs, you can rest assured that you will be able to get a rental car to drive while the repairs are being made. What this means to you is that you can avoid the hassle and humiliation of borrowing someone's car or asking for rides to work and elsewhere. This coverage provides you with a convenient alternative to being dependent on other people for a ride."

Because of the nature of price and product as factually based elements of value, the sales professional faces a much bigger challenge in translating these naturally cold, left-brain factors into emotionally stimulating language for the customer to hear and process.

Therefore, two irrefutable and immutable laws exist which directly concern price and product for the sales professional. These are:

1. **Never, never, never, NEVER state the price of something without connecting it to a benefit statement,** and
2. **Never, never, never, NEVER speak about product without translating its features into benefit(s) language!**

When a sales professional connects the price to the benefits of ownership, they are bridging the customer's left-brain thought processes to the emotional right-brain thought processes. The same is true when product features are linked to benefit rich language for the customer. Two completely dispassionate and unemotional factors of the sales process, price and product, must be translated to the emotional realm of a person's thought processes by connection to the benefits ('what's in it for me') they will realize if the sales professional is to be persuasive and compelling in the sales conversation.

To ignore such advice is to commit one of the most common sales mistakes in the industry. Don't be common.

The final two factors, or elements, that make up this idea of value are emotionally based in character. They are naturally right-brain functions, physically cohabitating with that part of our human psyche which sees the so-called big picture through visual stimulation, personal beliefs, emotions, imagination, and imagery in order to seek solutions to revealed problems and to make decisions.

The two elements I am referring to are you, the Person, the sales professional, expert; and the Place, the environment you create, such as the agency location or the Internet website or portal that forms the juncture or intersection at which the agent sells and the customer buys. Both of these factors present a strong emotional pull on the decision-making process of the customer to buy or not to buy. Their influence on the decision making process and a customer's impulse to buy is naturally more persuasive than price or product could ever be. Both the person and the place of the value equation stimulate a customer's right brain functions

Pull Your Nose Up

naturally. Both play an enormous role in the success or failure in a sales professional's ability to close a sale.

3) THE PERSON FACTOR

On closer examination of the person factor in the Value Diamond Concept, I refer to Dale Carnegie's observations about perceptions and the avenues by which people form opinions, feelings, and impressions about us. Carnegie stated that "every person is known and evaluated by four things and four things only: what we do, how we look, what we say, and how we say it."

Consider those occasions when you've been asked, "So, what is it that you do for a living?" Better yet, recall those times when you yourself have asked a similar question of someone.

Oh, I know that most of the time, our rationale for asking the question is born of polite curiosity and as a conversation starter, or at least that's what we tell ourselves. But what are the real motives behind such a question? Where does this 'polite curiosity' really come from?

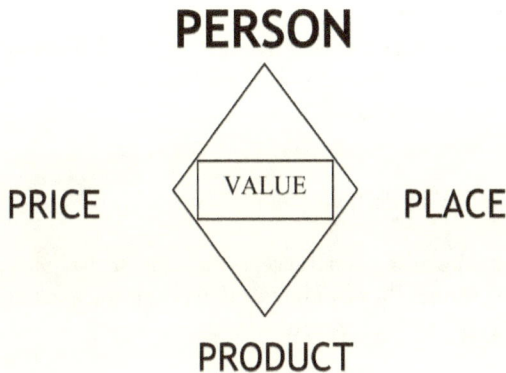

PERCEPTION IS REALITY, AND THE FACTS ARE IRRELEVANT

People are judgmental. They form opinions of us within seconds of a first encounter. It doesn't matter whether their opinion of you is accurate or if it is based on facts.

What does matter is that people form immediate opinions of other people upon initially meeting them. Acceptance of this basic fact about our nature as human beings and leveraging this knowledge will help you to close more sales and retain more customers.

If a customer's opinion about you is wrong after first meeting with you, that's irrelevant. What is relevant is the opinion they have formed of you. That opinion is what will become their reality, as well as their frame of reference, their baseline, for how they will react to you as an agent. It will also form the basis for whether they will decide to buy from you or not buy from you.

Perception is reality. The truth, the facts, accurate accounting—none of these things has anything to do with someone's initial perception of another person. Truth, of course, is important, and accurately representing the facts does matter, but strictly speaking of customer perceptions and what is real and important to the customer and what isn't, only perceptions matter, and nothing else.

What do people perceive of you? The answer will define what you need to change or work on in order to improve what customers see or perceive about you.

WHAT A CUSTOMER PERCEIVES IS WHAT MATTERS

The sooner a sales professional accepts the premise that perception is reality, the sooner they can move on to becoming a better sales professional and a better person to boot.

YOU, THE PERSON, ARE WORTH THE PRICE

Insurance sales professionals have a distinct advantage over

Pull Your Nose Up

their competition when they recognize how powerful perception can be in improving the entire sales process from marketing to communicating value effectively and persuasively.

For example:

"Today, I'm also trying to earn your business, Mr. Smith. If you choose our agency to take care of all your insurance and financial needs, my pledge to you is to be your personal advisor and expert in these matters and to do much of the worrying for you so you don't have to bother.

"I am your link to value, making sure your insurance dollars are spent in the most efficient manner as possible. Sure, you can buy auto and homeowners' insurance off of just about anybody who has a license. Please understand that I am not bragging when I say I'm not just anybody, Mr. Smith. I am a different kind of agent. Why? Because I keep my promises to my customers, and I will be there when you need me. As your agent, I'll work for you, dealing with the details that can often be confusing when an auto accident occurs, answering your questions when your kids begin to drive, working for you 24/7 so you don't have to concern yourself with those things.

"Other companies give you a 1-800 number and forget about you in voicemail messages, many times avoiding the responsibility of being your advocate, but that's not how we do business. If you need help or have a question, I'm always here for you and will gladly take the time to talk and meet with you whenever you like.

"In that sense, I'm worth it. That's the value I bring to folks like you, Mr. Smith. I care, and because of that, my customers value the relationship we have. Doesn't it make sense to have that kind of relationship?"

That's what we do as sales professionals (or what we *should* do as sales professionals) in one of the noblest industries a person can work in. That is added value, and you are worth the price people pay for your product and expertise.

By telling our story, using emotional language, understanding the impact of vocals and how we say things on the human psyche, and by being conscious of appearance and body language, we can evoke a positive emotional response within people that speaks to them from within saying, "I'd like to buy from this person."

That's the kind of sales professional everyone should aspire to become.

4) THE PLACE FACTOR

The fourth and final piece to the Value Diamond Concept is the Place, and for our purposes here, I will confine our discussion to a physical location such as an agency office—although what we discuss is applicable to a website or other Internet portal where business is transacted as well.

How is your agency environment perceived by customers and the community around you? Is it a place where customers are readily greeted and welcomed when they walk through the door? Is it inviting, with a reputation for expert service, caring people, and a staff that is always there for you when you need them?

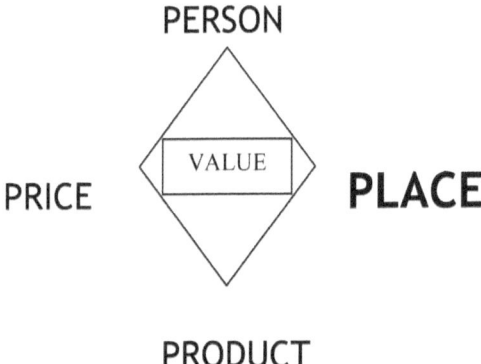

When is the last time you took a long, hard look at the physical condition or look of the exterior and interior of your office and asked yourself, "Is this the kind of place I'd want to invest my money?" If the answer to that question is something other than "Yes," changes need to be made.

ENVIRONMENT MATTERS IN PERCEPTION AND PERCEIVED VALUE

Environment matters and I don't just mean the physical surroundings. Yes, it's important to have a professional-looking and inviting office or place, but what of environment does the sales team create within the office? How are people greeted upon entering or when the telephone is answered by your staff? Are people welcomed as they walk in, and are giveaway gift items used during an appointment?

How easy is it to transact business with your staff? At every connection point of customer contact—call-in, walk-in, seminar, or appointment in the office—how can you make the customer feel valued, special, and important? The answer to that question can mean the difference between a good income and a great income for you.

What strategies do you employ to convey convenience, ease, and an overall pleasant experience for the customer when a call is taken on servicing issues? When an auto claim is filed, what's your strategy to relax the customer and engender confidence and loyalty toward you and the agency?

Marketing is not only about getting customers into the door and in front of you for a sales conversation. Marketing is also about keeping customers, so it behooves us as sales professionals to build a fence, of sorts, around our customers in order to block their defection by leveraging the goodwill of the agency (place) for cross-selling and up-sell opportunities.

THE VALUE DIAMOND: PRICE-PRODUCT-PERSON-PLACE

Anthony D. Cefalu

Value is a combination of a competitive Price, a quality Product, expert advice as the Person (or agent), and a Place where customers can comfortably transact business. This all comprises the idea of value… and that's what I call 'selling the whole package'!

Be Brilliant at the Basics

I was asked by a small business owner what I credit as the key to business success. He was just starting out in business, trying to manage a small sales force while managing the day-to-day activities of payroll, expenses, marketing, IT support, recruiting—all the moving parts that come with running a small business. After going through several business upstarts of my own, I knew exactly what he was feeling.

He was overwhelmed with all there was to do as a business owner, and his question was more of a plea to me to make some sense out of all the chaos that comes with small business ownership. He was stuck in a fog and needed help.

Immediately, I thought of a story I read about Vince Lombardi, legendary coach of the first Super Bowl Champion Green Bay Packers. Every year, at the start of practice, when the players returned to training camp in preparation for the start of the new season, Lombardi lifted a football high in the air for everyone to see and had this to say, "Gentlemen, this is a football."

What was that all about? He was speaking to a group of adults, wasn't he? These were grown men—big grown men! They were professional football players, not peewees getting ready for their first time on the field. These guys had been playing the game for a very long time... and for money, I might add. They were a part of an elite group of athletes who had made it to the top of their profession, a feat the vast majority of would-be professional players from all over the world could never boast of.

"Gentlemen, this is a football"? Surely they knew exactly what it was Coach Lombardi held in his hand, but what Lombardi was really trying to do was remind these professionals that it is important to maintain the basics. What the coach knew was that being brilliant at executing the fundamental skills or systems known to bring success is what matters most. What it takes to be successful is not elegant, nor is it overly clever or sophisticated.

In fact, the secret to being successful is very simple and basic. That was the lesson Lombardi was trying to teach to his men: Be brilliant at the basics, be the best you can be, and get serious about the fundamentals of the game, and success will follow as a result.

In the case of Lombardi's Packers, blocking, tackling, working as a team, and driving down the field, earning every yard with successful running and passing was what it took to be a champion. It wasn't glamorous work running and sweating in practice before each game, but it was honorable work, and it earned Lombardi and many of his players a place in history and induction into the National Football Hall of Fame—all for just being brilliant at the basics.

So, when my friend asked me, "What is the key to being successful?" I advised him of a couple of basic things he should consider in order to be successful in business—and in life, for that matter. All my recommendations centered on the following simple things, the basics of small business success.

* Marketing is all those things we do to get people in front of us, so spend the majority of your energy on that one task: getting people in front of you. How else will you get the opportunity to hold a sales conversation with anyone?

*Most marketing processes will center around two activities: looking for reasons to speak to people and looking for reasons

to meet with people. Most every marketing activity imagined by mankind will fall into either one of these two activities. Don't over think how to market. Just seek opportunities to speak and meet with people and build repeatable processes around these activities in order to regularly create opportunities to hold sales conversations with people. The reasons to speak with people and meet with people do not need to be favorable circumstances; they just need to be reasons.

* If marketing is all those things we do to get people in front of us, sales is what we do in front of people. Therefore, practice and rehearse, as sales is a little bit of theater. Make sure you know your lines.

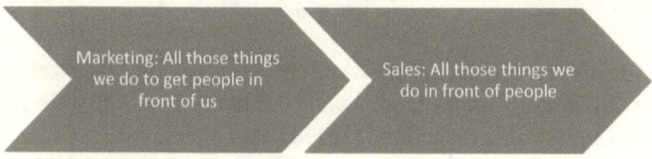

* Freedom regarding your time as a business owner is great, but freedom can kill some careers and businesses. Don't let the freedom of owning a business tempt you toward laziness.

People are only as lazy as they dare to be, and some people dare boldly. Use and enjoy your freedom as a business owner, but don't abuse it.

* You are not responsible for results. What you are responsible for is the right activities and processes to execute upon. Focus your energies not on the endgame results of production, sales, and income, but on the activities (processes) that give you production and income. Be brilliant with your marketing and sales processes, and the end result will take care of itself.

> You are Not Responsible for Results..
> You are Only Responsible for Right Activities

* Don't boil the ocean. Resist the urge to do everything at once, or else you will burn out. Build your business incrementally.

* The will to win is not as important as the will to plan to win. This is probably the most important piece of basic advice I can give. Be deliberate in what you do. Plan once, and then consider, reflect, and modify that plan and then put it into motion.

> The Will to Win is Not as Important
> as the Will to Plan to Win

* Ideas are a dime a dozen; it's their execution that is priceless. As the famous quote from a shoe company goes, "Just do it!" Put your words into action. The old Latin phrase *satis verborum* ("enough of words") *is* wise counsel for the agent-owner looking to go forward in their business rather than just survive.

* Successful people know their numbers. They have a line of

Pull Your Nose Up

sight to their goals. Are your goals within sight? Are you aiming in the right direction as a result? Do you know your numbers? For insurance and financial services agents, do you know your production, retention and persistency, closing ratio, return-on-investment, and expense ratio numbers, just to name a few? If not, you should… all the time.

* Peter Drucker, business expert, consultant, and one of the most respected minds in the entire business world is said to have stated, "The sole purpose of business existence isn't to make a profit… It is to create a customer." It doesn't get much simpler than that, my friends!

Do you want to be successful? Then take a lesson from what has been written here. I did not provide any specific secret formula for success, nor did I give you any step-by-step process to follow. What I did provide was some basic principles, some tenets to follow in order to build a foundation for business success.

Gentlemen (and ladies), this is insurance sales. Ignore me at your own peril.

Make the Best of the First Seven Seconds

I was in a store the other day—one I have frequented in the past—with the full intention of making a rather sizeable purchase.

THE DEPARTMENT STORE SALESPERSON

It was a Saturday around five fifty p.m. The first thing I noticed as I walked in was the salesperson's reaction upon seeing me. She flashed a glance my way and then quickly turned away in an attempt to disguise the fact that she knew I was there in the store. You know the look: She was hoping I didn't notice that she noticed me. Have you ever had that happen to you?

Then, with karate-like reflexes, she lifted her arm to chest level and frowned, staring down at her watch. It was clear to me what she was trying to signal to me through her body language: "We close in ten minutes, and I want to get home. Don't make me stay late."

My reaction to her body language was to do exactly what she wanted me to do: leave the store.

If running customers out of the store is one of the objectives of that salesperson, she was most successful. Yet, we all know it is absurd to think that is how a small business, or any business, should be run.

Anthony D. Cefalu

What can such behavior have on the ultimate survival of a business? How does inappropriate, unwelcoming employee behavior affect long-term profits, future sales, and viability in the marketplace?

It was apparent to me after gauging her behavior toward me that she was an employee of the business rather than an owner. Her actions betrayed her misunderstanding about the purpose of business and the ramifications of leaving that purpose unfulfilled (such as business failure and the subsequent loss of her job). As Peter Drucker said, "The purpose of business is to create a customer," and this is something we always must remember.

THE ATTORNEY'S OFFICE

I walked into an attorney's office and approached the receptionist. The professionally dressed woman was sitting behind the counter at a desk with her head down, staring at the desktop with a phone against her ear. Her conversation was imperceptible to me.

I stood there waiting respectfully, hoping she would acknowledge me in some fashion and note that I was present for an appointment, but she didn't notice me at all, or else she was just letting on that she didn't. This was somewhat infuriating because when I walked into the reception area, the opening of the entry door triggered a bell ring to alert her that a client was in the lobby, and I knew that even if she had not heard the bell, she most certainly had to see me walk up to her desk.

In much the same manner as with the department store salesperson who frowned at her watch, the receptionist knew I was there but didn't have the courtesy to acknowledge my presence and smile.

I realize that she could have been busy with a client of the firm and that patience is sometimes required—even of customers—in business settings, but what I am not willing to tolerate or accept is being ignored or made to stand there in an awkward moment. I was unsure of whether to sit or wait another humiliating minute until I was deemed important enough to be noticed, and it was blatantly clear to me that she did not care about how she made me feel.

A simple look up, a smile, a nod, a gesture with her hand indicating that she'd be with me in a moment would have sufficed and given her all the time she needed to take care of her business on the phone, but instead, she chose to make me feel unimportant and awkward; that is unforgivable for someone in business and unforgettable for the customer subjected to it.

THE DENTIST STORY

At my dentist's office, a notice is posted in the waiting room that reads:

Do Not Be Late to Your Appointment.

Those who are more than 10 minutes late must reschedule.

No Food Allowed in Waiting Area

No Cell Phone Usage

No More Than One Person to Accompany You in Waiting Area

I'm certain that the dentist or his staff could provide me with logical explanations for why they ask their customers not to be late, to reschedule, and not to bring food or cell phones into the small waiting room area, but before anything as callous and unfeeling as that sign is hung on the wall for customers to read and react to, the question of what the sign conveys to the customer should first be answered. It instantly makes the customer feel unwelcomed and 'lectured'... as if being at the dentist's office isn't already uncomfortable enough!

Anthony D. Cefalu

MY FAMILY DOCTOR

Though it is not my intent to pick on healthcare providers, it seems they are sometimes the biggest violators of poor marketing and poor salesmanship than most other small business owners.

Case in point, I had to make an appointment to see my doctor in the middle of the work day, meaning I had to take the time off against my vacation and sick days allotted by my employer. I didn't really have an issue with this, as those are the rules, but what I did have issue with was the sign in the office waiting room that read:

> It is called a waiting room for a reason.

I was stunned by the arrogance and presumptuous nature of such a sign, and it said so many things to me, none of which were any good.

FIRST IMPRESSIONS MATTER MORE THAN MOST BUSINESS PEOPLE THINK

Think particularly about the feelings you convey to people when they first walk into your office. Are you guilty of looking at your watch in disgust (figuratively, if not literally) as they enter in at the last minute of the business day? I know it's mentally challenging to have to deal with a customer at the end of a long, hard work day, as it's happened to all of us, but what good comes from making the customer feel any less for being there? What right does a sales professional have to make the customer feel awkward, for lack of a better term to describe the affect our insults have on them. It is shameful behavior to violate a customer's self-worth and dignity. Certainly, if it were to happen to you, you would feel wounded or angered with being ignored and made to feel awkward and unimportant. You wouldn't want to spend your money there, and if you treat your customers this way, they will not want to spend their money with you.

Pull Your Nose Up

Don't be guilty of treating customers negatively, no matter how subtle the act. Humans are very perceptive creatures, and first impressions matter. Thank your customers for coming in to your store or office. Acknowledge them when you see them in the community or right there at your place of business. Make them feel noticed and important by taking the time to recognize them and smile. Ask them how they are doing and guard against innocently insulting customers with careless words, subtle looks of disapproval, or by creating an environment that makes them feel threatened or belittled (such as posting callous or sarcastic signs).

Tune out the world and all its distractions and focus on your customers for that moment when they are in your storefront or office. Be present for them, aware of them and what they are saying. Get your customers thinking, "I like this person" or "I like this place and want to do business with these people." Chances are, they'll come back again and again, and they'll tell their friends to do the same.

MAKE THE BEST OF THE FIRST SEVEN SECONDS

It is a known fact that people make an average of eleven decisions about you in the first seven seconds of contact.

As for the attorney, I walked out the office and spent $2,000 on trust work for my family with a competitor of his just three doors down from that office. In the department store where we were ignored, I went to their competitor and bought all our furniture for our home and referred my sister, mother, and grandmother to them as well.

First impressions matter, folks! When it comes to your customers, make the best of the first seven seconds.

You Are the Missing Link

Value is realized when the customer makes the positive connection between price (premium) and the benefits to them of a product or service. Value is not necessarily a comparison or connection between a company's price and their competitors' prices. Instead, value is a relationship between several factors and the skillful art of the sales professional to communicate with the customer.

VALUE IS WHAT VALUE DOES

Value is a comparison of whatever your price *is* in connection to what your price does for the customer. It is the classic features-to-benefits discussion that top sales experts understand and apply to their craft as sales professionals. What the price *is* has no importance to the customer until they see what the price *does* for them—how something will benefit them. That is value.

Articulate the benefits. Don't fall into the trap of feeling compelled to compare your company or agency to the competition. If the customer brings up the subject of the competition, acknowledge it and move on in your discussion. Focus your sales conversation on how they will benefit by choosing you and your company relative to the price.

Get the customer looking *inside* rather than *outside* for a value comparison.

By this, I mean you must get the customer to internalize all the benefits of choosing your product and service—of how they will personally benefit—from doing business with you instead of anyone else. Get their mind's eye, away from looking outwardly at their current price and current insurance company for a frame of reference. Instead, get them looking inwardly at what you can do for them.

For that moment, ignore the price and concentrate on the customer's needs; articulate through illustration, stories, pictures, anecdotes, disturbing questions, and emotional language, placing the customer as the central character who will directly benefit from the miracle of insurance following an accident or health crisis.

TO BE UNDERSTOOD IS A LUXURY, AND IT TAKES WORK TO BE UNDERSTOOD

Do not worry about the price or the fact that a competitor is vying for the same customer. Instead, focus on clearly communicating what you mean to them as their insurance agent, their advisor. If and when the time comes when they need you to be there for them, keep your promise to your customer. Don't be like so many other agents and advisors who will say anything to get a sale; keep your promise to be there for them when they need you. That is value to a customer.

Price Is an Issue, but Who Has the Biggest Issue with Price?

Price will always be an issue, but I sometimes think it is more of an issue for the salesperson than it is for the prospect themselves. There is a strange phenomenon that occurs with agents when they are in a competitive situation, vying for a person's business against that of another agent.

The focus of the sales process quickly turns to price points and discount discussions rather than value. Consequently, agents

Pull Your Nose Up

eventually become sensitive to the differences they see when quoting prospects and feel almost apologetic when presenting a price that is higher than the competition.

Here is the reality: People do spend more money for seemingly similar products and services. Why? Because in some circumstances, they truly feel it is worth it. If you feel you are worth it, why worry about the price you have to quote?

JUST BECAUSE THE COMPETITION'S PRICE IS LOWER DOESN'T MEAN THEY ARE BETTER

When price is discussed, one value proposition is the value proposition of you, the agent. You are the missing link to value—the link that is all too often overlooked and undersold to customers, missing because of a failure to explain to people what you mean to them as their agent.

So, when the premium is stated or discussed, help the customer to understand the value they will be getting if they choose you as their agent, their advisor, a personal sales professional in the insurance and financial services industry. Do that, and they will be more likely to choose you for their insurance needs over someone else.

For example:

"As an expert in auto and homeowners' insurance, I deal specifically with the often complicated details associated with claims, billing, and the concerns and questions that naturally arise when people talk about protecting their cars and their homes—two of the biggest purchases most people ever make in their lives. It is important for you to have someone you can trust to answer your questions and do the worrying for you. That's what I do for people every day, 24/7.

"Have you ever had an automobile accident or homeowners' claim or known anyone who has? How did you deal with it? What were some of the difficulties you ran into while settling the claim? What part of the process was the most challenging or confusing for you? What were some of the difficulties you experienced during the process?

"How important would it be for you to have an advocate like me in your corner? How valuable would it be for you to have an expert taking care of all the details?

"You get the value of my experience of working with hundreds of people just like you, as their advisor in these matters. So while you're busy doing what you like, I'm the one worrying and working on your behalf, seeing that you and your family are properly protected and taken care of so you don't have to be distracted or spoil your family fishing trip.

"Other companies give you a 1-800 number and forget about you in what I call 'voicemail purgatory'—a seemingly endless tree of voice prompts and confusing pushbutton choices where you can't speak to a live human being about your problem. That won't happen at this agency. That's not how we do business. If you need help or have a question, I'm always here for you and will gladly take the time to talk and meet with you whenever you like… and if by some chance you do get our voicemail, our policy is to call back within twenty-four hours, often much sooner than that. In fact, here is my cell number in case you ever have a question and need to get in touch with me right away about an accident or a bill. Just dial that number, and I will answer.

"In that sense, I'm worth it. That's the value I bring to families like yours. I care, and because of that, my customers value the relationship we have. Doesn't it make sense to have that kind of relationship and trust with an agent? What do you think?"

YOU ARE THAT LINK TO VALUE

As an insurance professional, you don't sell insurance or financial products; you sell:

Pull Your Nose Up

Peace of mind
Trust
Confidence
Fulfilled promises
No worries

Security
Realized dreams
Access and availability
No hassles

You mean so much more to people than they realize, and the challenge for you is to get them to realize it.

You are that link to value. Without you as the agent and advocate for the customer, there is no value in the products and services you sell.

That said; make sure you tell people about who you are and what you can do for them. Let them know how valuable you are to them, or else they'll never know.

Success Is the Best Revenge

I was thirty-two years old, had just relocated to my childhood town of Youngstown, Ohio, married nine years and was the father of two young children: Lindsay at twenty-two months and Tony at eight months. The first Gulf War had just ended, and I was a brand new civilian, fresh off of a nine-year career as an Air Force officer.

It was my first day of work as an account executive (an agent) with one of the largest life insurance companies in the country. I had never sold a thing in my life. I went from career soldier to insurance salesman, and I will admit it was a very uncertain time for me and my family.

Part of my introduction into the company was a quick tour of the branch office I would be working out of while selling life, health, investment, auto, and homeowners' insurance. It was a bland office, very sterile and not stylish at all. It was the kind of office where one would expect to get work done and nothing more, a completely Spartan atmosphere. There were five or six smaller interior offices reserved for the top producers in the branch and approximately fifteen cubicles for those who had yet to earn such a distinction. My cubicle was in the back of the office.

As I was being introduced to the staff, one agent, a young and recognized top producer, took the opportunity to pull me aside to share with me some friendly advice about the insurance business. "You're Number 41," he said.

"Excuse me?" I asked, befuddled.

"You're Number 41," he repeated. "I've seen forty come, and I've seen forty go. So like I said, you're Number 41."

My response back to him can't be published. Afterward, I walked to my cubicle thinking about what had happened, and I took a piece of paper out of the desk and wrote on it, '#41' and pinned it to the cubicle wall.

Every time I sat in my cubicle to print a proposal, work up a quote, or use my phone, I saw that piece of paper and could hear that guy saying, "You're Number 41." It made me angry, but it inspired me to excel. Nine months later, I was accepting the company award for top producer in sales. In less than a year, I had out-produced hundreds and hundreds of agents, some with as many as forty years of sales experience to their credit.

There were a lot of reasons why I was able to accomplish what I did in such a short time. I planned out each work day, kept my focus on executing my marketing plan, scripted out my sales conversations, tracked all my sales, and made sure nothing got hung up in underwriting. There were other factors that helped as well, albeit it nothing unique or unusual. My success came down to working as hard and as smart as I could to hit my production goals.

I also had a great manager for whom I will ever be indebted for his guidance, encouragement, and solid sales training. He was instrumental in making my introduction into the industry a positive experience, and he took the time to share with me the benefit of his years of sales experience and expertise.

Still, the person I am most grateful to is the young agent who branded me 'Number 41'. Because of him, I was inspired to succeed and not fail. In life, there will always be people who tell you what you can and can't do. They will try to limit you in what you can accomplish by the words they use against you. They are negative

Pull Your Nose Up

people, small-minded individuals you need to stay away from, or else you might begin believing what they say about you.

The old cliché that we are our own worst critics is true. There will always be personal doubts and circumstances that plague us, and we will occasionally question our own abilities to succeed and achieve things. It is a struggle against the environmental forces of life on the outside that tell us we won't succeed and the personal doubts about our own abilities to succeed that most people quietly harbor inside their hearts and minds. It's a normal part of the human condition.

The lesson I learned from being Number 41 was this: You can choose to accept the estimates negative people make of you, or you can choose to prove them wrong. You can let that quiet, small voice that causes you to doubt your own chances to succeed convince you that it is true, or you can put it to rest and muzzle it for good by staying focused on your goal and accomplishing what you set out to accomplish.

I despised the agent who called me Number 41. I despised him for what he said and thought of me as a person, but I despised him even more for the fact that he might have been right—that he might have validated my own self-doubts about my potential for success as an agent simply by that dreaded nickname.

I could have gotten revenge against that guy in a lot of different ways, but that would have been wrong. Instead, it was my success as an agent that was ultimately the best revenge, and it was one of the best lessons I have ever learned in life.

Success is the Best Revenge

Success quiets your critics and proves them wrong about their low opinion of your capabilities… and it extinguishes self-doubt and puts steel in your resolve to achieve things in the future.

What about you? You may not have someone telling you that success is reserved for others and not you, but if you are like most people, you probably struggle with some degree of self-doubt. Whatever your situation, are you getting your revenge? Are you muzzling the quiet voice inside of you that says, "You can't do it"?

Don't live with the weight of doubt and criticism about your chances to succeed. Silence the critics—especially those in your own mind. Refuse to succumb to estimates and predictions of your failure. Get your revenge by making your own success. It is the best feeling in the world.

By the way, after I was awarded the distinction of salesman of the year by the company, I was granted a private office within the branch for being a top producer. The office I was offered was that of the agent who had dubbed me Number 41. Success is the best revenge, and there is nothing like it!

How Often Has this Happened to You?

"The deepest principle in human nature is the craving to be appreciated." ~ William James, Launching a Leadership Revolution

Imagine entering a building such as a mall or some type of office, and as you open the door to enter, you notice someone walking toward you to exit the building by the very same doorway you are going to enter. Out of thoughtfulness and good manners, you defer to them and hold the door open, giving them the right-of-way while you patiently wait... and wait... and wait.

What is it that you are waiting for? Of course! A "Thank you" from the passerby. But sometimes, there is no gratitude, and they just walk on through the open door. In fact, they may not even acknowledge you and avoid eye contact, pretending you aren't even there. It is as if they expected you to hold it open for them.

After they pass, you enter the building secretly telling yourself, "Oh, it's no big deal. I'm above needing gratitude. I'm the better person," but inevitably, you begin to think, "How rude of them to not say 'Thank you'. Where are their manners? I just can't understand some people. Common courtesy is not so common anymore, I suppose."

Anthony D. Cefalu

THE EXCHANGE OF MONEY IS NEVER AN UNEMOTIONAL EVENT FOR A CUSTOMER

It is an awful feeling not to be appreciated or recognized for a good deed. If something as simple and seemingly innocent as failing to say "Thank you" for an open door can trigger such negative feelings (and rightfully so), consider how people feel when we miss the opportunity to thank them whenever we do business with them at the agency.

Let me say it again: In everything we do, our actions are largely driven by our emotions and supported later by logic. This is especially true for our customers.

Never let them feel unappreciated or taken for granted, or worse yet, taken advantage of by not being shown courtesy when they deal with you. Whenever you conduct business with customers, take heed of these reminders in order to properly show them you appreciate their patronage while also avoiding the offense of making them feel taken advantage of:

When they call in about a question on their bill…

Say, "Thank you. We appreciate your business and remember, whenever you need anything, we're here for you. Have a nice day."

When they refer a friend to you…

Say, "Thank you for recommending us. We appreciate your referral and are happy to give them the same care we provide to you. We've sent you a little something in the mail in appreciation for your confidence in us. Thanks again."

When they call with a complaint…

Say, "We apologize for the inconvenience we've caused you and thank you for calling and giving us a chance to correct things for you. We value you as a customer. Without talking to you,

Pull Your Nose Up

we wouldn't be able to fix the problem for you or avoid this ever occurring again, so we appreciate you contacting us. Thanks again."

When they call with a compliment or praise…

Say, "Thank you! That is very kind of you. It's so important to us to make sure we are here for you. You can rest assured we are doing the worrying for you regarding your insurance needs so you don't have to. Thank you again."

When they suggest things you can do or make a comment on how things can be improved…

Say, "Thank you. We keep a ready ear for ways to improve the way we do business, and it is people like you whose opinions matter the most to us. I appreciate you sharing that with us and will make sure we discuss it in one of our team meetings."

When they comply with your request for something…

Say, "Thank you for bringing in the paperwork we needed for your jewelry. I understand you are busy and realize how tough it can be to get time off of work to bring something in to the office. That is going to help a lot when it comes to protecting your items and to give you peace of mind much quicker than if we had to wait for it in the mail."

Whenever they come into the office…

Say, "Thank you for taking the time out of your busy day to meet with me to discuss your life insurance needs. Knowing how important this is to so many families like yours, I applaud you for making this a priority for your family."

When they wait patiently… and not so patiently…

Say, "Thank you for waiting. I really do appreciate it. We don't take your time lightly and do apologize for the wait."

When they do business with you… every time!

Say, "Thank you. I really appreciate your business. Knowing that you have many choices, we do thank you for choosing us as your insurance agent."

Courtesy and good manners are a lost social art. It is all too commonplace to experience ingratitude, to not be appreciated and made to feel special. Remember, although each of us is unique and different in many ways, we're also very similar as well. To be valued and appreciated is a shared craving and one of the greatest of human desires. Help yourself by remembering to say "Thank you" to your customers when you meet them and transact business with them. They will be more loyal and will keep coming back as a result.

If you don't think it matters, just think how much you appreciate it when you, as a customer, are thanked… or not thanked.

Fail to give customers what they want, and they will go somewhere else where they can get it.

Hire for the Position, Not the Person

RECRUITING, HIRING, AND FIRING: IT COMES WITH THE TERRITORY

Recruiting, interviewing, hiring, executing background checks, training, and integrating individuals into capable business associates is an undeniable function within all business entities, no matter how small. The agent-owner who effectively and economically executes their role in these areas will be the business entity that survives another day in fulfilling the business purpose of creating new customers.

Those who get lost in the hiring process or get bogged down by uncertain recruiting costs and high expenses involved with installing new hires into the organization simply will not survive.

In order to remain viable as a business entity and to sustain growth, agent-owners must constantly scout for talent while at the same time remain ready to assess the potential of a candidate's fitness to fill a given position. Thus, it is extremely important for the agent-owner to draft detailed job descriptions for each position within the organization, detailing all functions within the agency that fall under the requirements of the position before ever considering recruiting and hiring someone.

Consider the integration of new talent into an agency and the expense associated with the process. The cost involved with the acquisition of talent and the time invested in evaluating each potential hire can be heavy. It can also be expensive from a production standpoint.

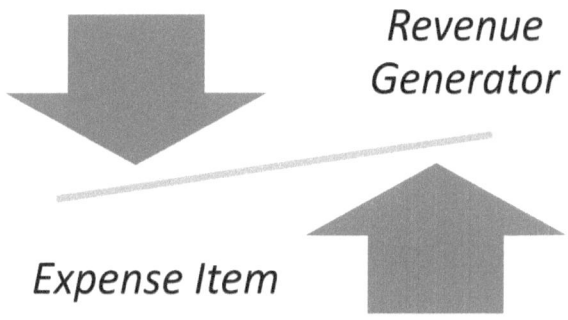

The great challenge facing agent-owners is hiring staff who will serve as *revenue generators* as opposed to *expense items* on the balance sheet at the end of the year.

HOW DO I INCREASE MY CHANCES OF HIRING A PROFITABLE EMPLOYEE?

What can an agent or small business owner do to increase the likelihood that a new hire will be a revenue generator for them rather than another expense item to worry about? The best thing an agent can do is to be deliberate and disciplined in the hiring process; deliberate in hiring for the position and not the person and disciplined with adhering to such a process.

What often happens in the hiring process is this: Agent-owners, in an attempt to circumvent the hard work of selecting the right talent for their business, often take an expedient and seemingly painless hiring path by finding and hiring someone who has worked in the insurance industry in the past or has an insurance license. The ensuing interview can be summarized by one almost desperate question asked by the agent to the candidate: "Do you have any experience or insurance licenses?"

If the answer to the question is in the affirmative, a job offer will be tendered, proving the allure that hiring experience and licenses has over the discipline of hiring the right person for the position instead. The logical justification for such a selection process is, "I don't have to wait for them to get—or worse yet, pay for them to get—a license or learn agency processes." That kind of thought process is a mistake too often made by agent-owners.

WHEN HIRING TALENT, EXPEDIENCY IS A RECIPE FOR DISASTER

This same weak logic can be likened to, "Do you have a driver's license, and have you any experience in driving a car? You do? Great. Congratulations! You are the newest member of our racing team. When can you start?"

Sound ridiculous? Yes it does! It's about as ridiculous as some of the recruiting and hiring practices being used today by many agents.

Experience, licenses, and a likability factor are important aspects to consider during the selection phase in hiring a person, but these should not be the sole factors considered.

Remaining disciplined in your approach to recruiting and evaluating talent is vital in matching the right candidate for the position at hand. The proper way to evaluate talent is against a standard based on the skill sets necessary to perform the functions of the position.

Anthony D. Cefalu

> HELP WANTED
> Race Car Driver
>
> Local racing team in need of a winning race car driver. We are a high-performance racing team looking for a winning driver who gets results.
>
> If you have a driver's license and have ever driven a car at any time in your life, apply today.

Hire for the position, not the person.

JOB DESCRIPTIONS & MATCHING THE REQUIREMENTS OF THE POSITION TO THE PERSON

Being *disciplined* in the hiring process means deliberately matching the skills and abilities of a candidate with the detailed tasks as outlined in the job description. This process helps prevent the agent-owner from relying on the uncertain factors of personality and industry experience when assessing a candidate's fitness for an agency staff position. Instead, it allows the agent-owner to focus on specific competencies and skill sets as outlined in the job description.

The candidate who is hired for what they can do rather who they are has the greater likelihood of being a good hire. This person will generate revenue instead of creating expense. In contrast, an unstructured and random selection process can only result in the wrong person being hired, and this, quite literally, has a cost all its own.

Pull Your Nose Up

HIRE FOR THE POSITION & OTHER WORDS OF WISDOM TO CONSIDER

Hiring for the position and not the person is a philosophy that can save the agent-owner a lot of time and money in reduced acquisition, training, and costs for the agency.

Hiring for the position and not the person will also save the agent-owner the heartache and anguish associated with firing an associate who under-performs and who was never a fit for the job in the first place.

Hiring for the position and not the person will save the agent-owner from the possible dilemma of keeping the wrong person on the company payroll—a very costly problem for any business owner.

Hiring for the position and not the person objectifies the selection process and allows the agent-owner to focus on each potential candidate for what they can do in light of specific skill requirements outlined in the job description. That kind of disciplined focus in the hiring process reduces the likelihood of picking the wrong candidate due to biases that can cloud one's judgment when a final selection is made.

Hiring for the position reduces the likelihood of what I call 'falling in love with a candidate' from occurring. What that means for the agent-owner is this: On occasion (more times than I would like to remember), I have witnessed agent-interviewers becoming entranced and obvious in their favor for a particular candidate while the actual interview is transpiring. Candidates notice this behavior, as do colleagues in the interview. The only person who doesn't notice this is happening is the one exhibiting the behavior. It's an unprofessional and embarrassing moment when it occurs, and in some instances, it is disturbing. Also, such behavior never leads to a hire based on the ability of the candidate to fulfill the requirements of the position. Instead, it can lead to an added expense—the equivalent of a divorce. At a minimum, it places the interviewee in a position of advantage when it comes to salary and benefits negotiation. So much for expense management.

Hiring for the position and not the person allows the interviewer to focus on other elements of the candidate's suitability for the job. These might include attitude, ability, and professional appearance. Personally, those are factors that weigh heavier in my final hiring decision versus the experience and licensing issues other agents consider.

Job Description

Customer Service Representative

Must have strong telephone skills, computer skills, and the ability to process multiple transactions quickly and accurately. Additionally, the position is a customer-facing role, requiring the candidate to effectively deal with customer complaints, questions, and requests on a daily basis.

Required competencies for success include:

* The ability to make daily outbound appointment calls to set insurance and financial services sales appointments for agency sales representatives.
* The effective utilization of local computer platforms to create and manage lists of current clients and new prospective clients.
* The ability to accurately and independently process payments on a daily basis by phone and/or in person from walk-in clients by following specific agency procedures and methods.

In summary, be deliberate in how you seek and acquire new employee talent. Focus your efforts on hiring for the position and not the person. Using a detailed job description as your guide

Pull Your Nose Up

and standard in determining an individual's suitability for the position is the best place to start when assessing candidates.

Be disciplined in your approach as well. Adhere to a determined and strict process of objectivity by carefully gauging a candidate's abilities and potential against the job description. This will enable you to avoid unnecessary expense and emotional distress that would otherwise result from a hiring process that ignores the requirements of the position needing filled.

You Are Not Responsible for Results

If you have been in the sales profession for any length of time, no doubt you have come across the following time-honored quote, either on a motivational poster in a sales training room or during a pep talk meant to energize the sales force:

Don't Mistake Activity for Results
You are Paid for Results, Not Activity

The point of the quote is that just busying oneself about the sales profession doesn't yield sales results, and that is quite true, but I would much rather we adopt the following quote instead:

You Are NOT Responsible for Results
You ARE Responsible for Right Activities
Right Activities = Right Results
Right Results = Sales Success

One of the most difficult things for the sales professional to maintain is perspective. In fact, it is perspective that can sustain a successful sales career or submarine it, cutting it short from what could have been a promising and fulfilling lifelong endeavor.

When I first met Susan, she was an energetic twenty-five-year-old that had never sold anything before. I had left my agency and direct sales for an opportunity to join one of the biggest insurance and financial services institutions in the United States. My work at that time focused on the training and development of new agency sales professionals and life sales specialists within the organization.

Susan was one of those sales professionals, eager to learn and get started, coachable, and very motivated. She was the kind of student-sales professional that anyone would love to work with and get to know.

When her training period with me ended, she was sent out to do the work she was trained to do—to sell life, auto, and homeowners' insurance. And sell she did! Susan quickly distinguished herself as one of the top sales professionals in the company. Among nearly 400 of her peers, Susan was in the top 10 percent when it came to sales results. She was a success—at least early on.

Over time, though, I noticed a change in Susan. Not only did her sales numbers plummet, but her attitude and demeanor was no longer energetic or glowing as it had been when we first began working together.

So one day, we got the opportunity to talk about her career and her work. She recounted for me how difficult it was for her to stay focused and motivated. There was so much to do, and the pressure of that coupled with meeting sales production quotas was weighing her down. Her income from bonuses was also declining every week that went by as her sales production decreased.

As I sat there and listened to her chronicle the struggles of the business of sales, I recalled my own experiences and lessons. I had been like her once: energetic and eager to succeed, focused on sales results, running a mile a minute without light at the end of the tunnel, and profoundly hurt on an emotional level when a sale wasn't made or was dismantled for one reason or another. So, I knew what Susan's problem was: perspective.

I began to ask Susan the following questions:

"What is it you think you are responsible for, Susan?"

Pull Your Nose Up

"Sales."

"Okay. Help me to understand how you are responsible for sales."

"Well, I have to sell a certain number of policies every month to meet quota, or else I get in trouble—not to mention I don't make as much money. That's how I'm responsible for sales."

"But if you are responsible for something, doesn't it make sense that somewhere in the process, you must have control over that thing for which you are responsible?"

She responded, "I guess so. What are you trying to say?"

I asked further, "Do you have control over whether a person buys from you or not?"

"Well, yes," she said.

"How?"

"By effective communication, compelling sales presentations, and regular marketing," she replied.

"I can appreciate you saying that, but those are processes and systems—things you control. How is it you have control over whether the customer buys from you or not? I'm speaking here in regard to their impulse to buy."

She replied, "I don't control the customer's impulse to buy. I can try to influence it, but ultimately, I can't get into their head and make them buy from me. If I could, I would," she said jokingly.

"Precisely," I said. "So why do you anguish over a customer who doesn't buy from you? If you can't control their impulse to buy, why take it so personally when they don't?" I continued, "Why not focus your energies, your attention, on those areas of the sales process you *can* control? Why waste precious energy, resources, and your own mental wellbeing worrying about things you cannot control? Susan, is it possible for a sales professional to sell every single person they present to?"

She answered, "No."

"Of course not! So why expect the unattainable from yourself? Why punish yourself mentally? Every sales professional has their ups and downs, their big weeks and slow weeks. It happens. We have to accept it as the nature of our profession. But instead, you know what I see a lot of times when I work with agents like yourself? I see them focusing on hitting quota and taking responsibility for results they really have no direct control over. How absurd is that?"

SALES HERESY OR SALES GENIUS? YOU DECIDE

"Susan, this may come as a shock to you. It may even sound like sales heresy to you when I tell you, but you are NOT responsible for results. You, Susan, are responsible for right activities, or right behaviors, if you like. You are responsible for establishing regular and systematic marketing systems.

You are also responsible for executing those processes completely, regularly, and often. You are responsible for practicing and perfecting your sales presentation. You are responsible for tracking your results and setting goals. You are responsible for creating a sales environment favorable to making the sale. You are even responsible for being disciplined and repeating those activities that yield results over time. But you are not—and I repeat, you are **NOT**—responsible for the results themselves. Those you cannot control. And I promise you this, Susan… if you perform the right activities and concentrate your own energies toward tasks and measures known to create sales success, you'll be happier and more successful. You'll make this a lifelong career instead of another job listed on a checkered resume."

I encouraged Susan to listen to my counsel because what I know

Pull Your Nose Up

is, many new sales professionals fail due to having the wrong perspective about what it takes to be successful. I was once like many other new sales professionals. I had the perspective that the sale depended all on me and only me. If someone didn't buy, I took it personally—very personally. Over time, those lost sales began to look more and more like failure to me.

Soon, I was defining myself as a failure in my own heart. I began to doubt my abilities and my decision to be in the sales profession. Ultimately, I grew increasingly unhappy and unmotivated. It wasn't until I learned that I had the wrong perspective that I started improving my production results, as well as my entire attitude toward the business.

Instead of worrying about the next sale, we must think about what we can control. I asked Susan, "What is it you can control, Susan?"

She said, "My activities—what I do every day in the office to get people in for an appointment."

Susan was exactly right. It is important to understand that reality and to keep a healthy perspective on what you actually can do to improve on your business results.

I encouraged Susan to try an experiment that may work for you, too, if you find yourself feeling responsible for results. Assume the perspective that right activities will yield right results; maybe not immediately, but eventually they will yield sales for you. For the next several weeks, focus your energies on getting those marketing and sales processes right and pay less attention (or focus) on getting the sale.

I told Susan to "See what happens and let me know what you think."

"Okay. I'll do that."

I knew that if Susan stuck with the pledge of concentrating the majority of her attention, energy, and problem solving on the execution of sound marketing processes and principles, the sales would eventually start to come, and her results would pick up and take her out of her slump.

I was also concerned for her mental health. All too often, I meet burned out, bitter sales agents who have gotten to the place of desperation merely because they allowed the perverted notion of being responsible for the results to weigh heavy on their minds, egos, and overall health.

As a result, many agents leave the profession, or in the very least become jaded individuals who are no longer in tune with the original reason why they got into the business in the first place: to help other people in one of the noblest of pursuits a man or woman can ever engage in.

THE LESSON IN HAVING THE RIGHT PERSPECTIVE ON THE SALES PROFESSION

When you've had a tough week and sales are down, reflect on your activities. Ask yourself, "Did I do all those things I know to do in order to make the sale, in order to be successful?"

If the answer is "Yes," you can put your head upon your pillow at the end of such a week and say to yourself, "It just wasn't my week. I did all I could. But tomorrow's coming, and I know, over time—maybe over the course of a month or a year—I'll be able to look back and say I had a good year overall. Yes, there were some low points and some high points in my sales calendar, but overall, by staying disciplined at right activities, I had a great year of sales production."

YOU END UP WHERE YOUR EYES ARE FOCUSED

Having the perspective that you are not responsible for results, but instead, are responsible for right behaviors and activities, will serve you well in the long run.

Keep your eyes focused on your activities. Be cognizant of where you are with your sales numbers. Stay focused in applying your best efforts toward those activities, those processes that revolve around marketing and getting people in front of you and then think about the selling part, what you do in front of people.

Keep your eyes pointed in the right direction. Your mental health and professional success relies on this advice.

You Are NOT Responsible for Results
You ARE Responsible for Right Activities
Right Activities = Right Results
Right Results = Sales Success

As the rest of the story goes, Susan made a turnaround in her sales production. Never did I see her so down on herself again. Of course she experienced the inevitable slumps here and there in her production, but at the close of every year, she finished in the top 10 percent of her peers—on a national level at that! She has since moved up in the organization as a sales manager and is now an executive who continues to coach and lead others to success. And as for her glow, her smile, and her captivating energetic nature, they are back in full force. Why? Because she learned that she was not responsible for results!

Slow to Hire, Quick to Fire

Hire for the position slowly and fire for the position quickly. The hiring process does not have to be a quick process, but it does need to be a deliberate process, whereby the agent thoughtfully considers candidates in light of the job requirements.

Avoiding the hiring rush will ensure that the best candidate is selected. Agent-owners seem to understand this concept, but it is the quick to fire concept that they struggle with the most.

RELUCTANCE TO FIRE SOMEONE IS A GOOD THING... AND A BAD THING

Agents hate to fire people; that's a good thing and a bad thing. Reluctance to fire is *good* from the standpoint that firing an individual should never be taken lightly. Anytime the termination of an individual's livelihood is considered, it is a serious matter and should, therefore, only be done strictly for business reasons only and after careful consideration.

THE DECISION TO FIRE SOMEONE IS A BALANCING ACT

The employee who should be fired and is not will continue to be a tremendous burden on the profitability of an agency operation. This is a *bad* thing for the agent-owner and for the overall health and stability of the business operation. Waste is always a foolish thing, and in any business venture, the wasting of precious capital resources on an inefficient employee can be a death toll.

The decision to fire someone is a balancing act between the performance of the employee and the business needs of the agency or business organization.

When you hire for the position and not the person, firing an individual becomes more of an objective matter versus an emotional one. I am not suggesting that firing someone should be easy, but when a person is hired for the position, there is an expectation set with the job description that is undeniable to the employee. In such instances, being quick to fire is less of an emotional burden for both the agent-owner and the employee.

Fail your failures fast. The longer you keep an under-performing employee on the payroll, the more money they take from you and your business. Don't give your money away! It's not dignified, and it is a foolish thing to do.

In a marketplace where revenues are difficult to capture and expenses are so easily incurred, hiring talent into the business operation is an unsettling prospect for most business owners. The very process of hiring someone into the agency can be an expensive venture, placing a drag on precious cash reserves and business investments.

Do yourself a favor and avoid the mistakes that create an expense nightmare for the average agent-owner: Hire for the position and not the person, and be slow to hire and quick to fire when it comes to an under-performing employee.

You'll thank me for this advice, and so will your employees—even the under-performing employee who is honest in assessing their own inability to get the job done.

Off to a Good Start, But with No End in Sight

"Ninety percent of the game is half mental." ~ *Yogi Berra*

Marathon runners are a very special breed of people. Why? Because of the limits they push their bodies in a 26.2 mile race—limits that not only test the endurance of the human body, but also the power of the will to go on despite the mind's rejection of the endeavor and the spirit's despair at the daunting task of a finish line unseen.

At what mile mark do most runners quit a marathon? You might guess the fifth or tenth mile, when the finish line seems so far away and the body is beginning to anticipate the excruciating pain to come. But like most things in life, a seemingly simple matter such as the question of when most runners quit running in a marathon race is not as easily answered as you might think.

RUNNING A RACE? A GOOD START IS CRUCIAL

Aside from the first mile, the twenty-sixth is when the least amount of people quit the race. I think the reason this is true stems from a simple explanation of line of sight, or vision for the finish line, where the power of the mind can push the body beyond normal physical limits by way of a clear goal toward the future.

Anthony D. Cefalu

It is important to get off to a good start at the beginning of a race. If a person is to have any chance of success at something, a clear mental picture of the end is very important to when it comes to staying strong and committed, no matter the challenge or the goal. So the beginning of a task (such as the first mile in a 26.2 mile marathon) witnesses very few people quitting because a runner's vision of the finish line is so fresh and untested.

Most runners don't quit at the first mile or so of a marathon because of fresh line of sight to the goal, and most marathon runners don't quit during the final mile either because they have a vision of where they are going—a tangible, palpable, real vision they can actually see. Sure, they are physically exhausted, but their vision fuels them and tells them to keep going to reach their destination, their prize.

IF THERE IS NO END IN SIGHT, THERE'S NO END IN SIGHT

So, what's the answer to our question? Most runners quit a marathon at the twentieth mile, a rather strange point to be quitting, it seems. Think of the personal investment made by the runner up to this point, all the pain, tolerance, and sheer willpower to keep going just to stop short of the finish line. Why? I think the answer goes back to the original discussion of vision and having a clear line of sight to the goal.

WHEN WE LOSE SIGHT OF THE PRIZE, QUITTING MAKES SENSE

When we lose sight of the prize, we lose sight of our purpose and motivation to continue. If there is no end in sight for the runner, there is nothing to be achieved or gained by continuing to try.

This happens even though a person may be invested both physically and mentally in a given endeavor, even invested to the point at which it seems impossible to ever want to give up. When goals fade away and a vision for the future dissipates, no measure of personal power will sustain the effort to move forward and take another step.

"Where there is no vision, the people perish." The Bible

This underscores an important principle that is a key to success, health, and happiness. That important principle is this: You must keep your vision alive and stay mentally, emotionally, and spiritually fit in order to prosper as an agent, a business owner, a spouse, a parent, and a member of the community. Know your business plan and envision for yourself what it is you want your agency or small business to be known for and remembered for when you are at the end of your career.

After all, there will be days when your fatigued body will say "No" when your mind has to say "Yes." There will be times when it seems everything in life conspires to sabotage your goals and dreams. And there will be weeks—or even months—when you feel like you are hitting the twentieth mile. Don't stop! Keep your eye on the vision *of what you want for your business and for your family.*

MAINTAIN YOUR VISION, AND YOU WILL SUSTAIN SUCCESS

The answer to running the race is to maintain your vision and focus on the finish line. Keep your vision alive, and it will keep you alive. Don't give up. Keep striving toward the vision planted in your mind and heart.

There is a simple three-step process to keeping your vision alive:

1. **Write it Down.** Write down your vision for your life and career. I once heard someone say, "If you think it, ink it!" and that's good advice. Agents who force themselves to write down their goals end up accomplishing those goals more readily than if they hadn't.

2. **Know your WHY.** Why is this vision significant to you? What do you hope for? What is the bigger reason for your vision? Your

why is your purpose. You must know your purpose in life. Trying to have vision without purpose is like trying to drive a car without an address for your destination; you'll be going nowhere fast and wasting gas along the way.

3. **Review your WHY Weekly or Daily.** Remember, if you keep your vision alive, it will keep you alive.

Purpose fuels your vision, and it fuels you. Write down your WHY, and your vision for the future will stay clear.

Don't Be a Half-Brained Sales Professional

People are both logical in nature and emotional. That is to say, our brains are constructed in such a manner that the left brain and right brain (the two distinct anatomic halves) function differently; they are each designed for specific tasks and processes and naturally adhere to them.

The left brain seeks details, facts and figures, and the literal interpretation of things. The right brain, on the other hand, is quite different in its function.

It is in the right brain that our intuitive senses reside. It is the retreat for all our feeling, fears, and beliefs. The right brain is the seat of our emotional being and is, therefore, the domicile of our impulse to act and to buy.

EMOTIONS AND THE IMPULSE TO BUY: INTERCONNECTED RIGHT-BRAIN FUNCTION

Whereas the left brain analyzes things, the right brain understands, empathizes, decides, and is moved to action. Together, the left and right brain form all our thoughts and behaviors as human beings. When the decision is made to buy something (a right-brain process), the planning and organizing needed to accomplish the act is processed in the left brain.

Anthony D. Cefalu

"These two minds, the emotional and the rational, operate in tight harmony for the most part... In many or most moments, these minds are exquisitely coordinated; feelings are essential to thought, thought to feeling. But when passions surge, the balance tips: it is the emotional mind that captures the upper hand, swamping the rational mind." (Daniel Goleman, *Emotional Intelligence*)

Customers feel first and think second. This statement is not meant to be an indictment against customers. Instead, it is simply recognition of how people process information and react to emotional appeals or stimuli.

According to Janelle Barlow, author of *Emotional Value*, "Emotions influence every aspect of our thinking life: they shape our memories; they influence our perceptions, our dreams, thoughts, and judgments, and our behaviors, including our decisions whether to return to a place of business, how much we are willing to pay for a product or service..."

Medical science and marketing research have proven that the customer mind, in relation to the buying behavior, is anything but completely logical. A clear hierarchy exists in our thinking; we buy on feeling or emotions and rationalize our behavior afterwards with facts.

"The intuitive gut feeling is the engine of the decision train, and logic and rationale are the cars it pulls behind. Yet in many of our presentations to clients we spend too much time filling the rationale boxcars with facts and figures and not enough time trying to influence the engine that pulls the train—the gut feeling. A powerful presentation first influences the emotion that drives the decision and then adds logic as the client asks for it ... Buying decisions hinge more on feeling than they do on fact." (Scott West and Mitch Anthony, *Storyselling for Financial Advisors*)

So what does this all mean to the sales professional? It means that in order to sell well, the sales professional must get emotional with customers.

Pull Your Nose Up

HOW TO GET EMOTIONAL WITH CUSTOMERS

What does it mean to get emotional with someone? In order to improve your sales, you must learn to speak and communicate in the language of the right brain.

Don't be a half-brained sales professional—the kind that is always appealing to the logic of the left brain! If you only feel comfortable within the realm of facts and are all too eager to explain to the customer the internal rate of return of a whole life insurance contract versus a universal life policy, you might have to step out of your comfort zone to be successful in sales.

It is important to be honest and factual with your customers, as that's part of being a sales professional, but for the sake of your professional sales career, and for the sake of the customer who is seeking clarity, understanding, guidance, and simplicity, be emotional in your sales conversations.

Don't confuse the customer with a bunch of facts and figures. This can be mentally and physically overwhelming and taxing on any individual. Besides, being technical and demonstrating your knowledge of every detail of a product does not bridge the mind to the emotional right brain, where the impulse to buy resides.

"There is no expedient to which a man will not resort to avoid a real labor of thinking." (Sir Joshua Reynolds, *Influence*)

Make the sales conversation as easy to understand as possible, while at the same time understanding that emotions rule our desires and impulses to buy.

For example:

"You know, Tom and Mary, waiting to buy this life insurance protection when you feel you are ready is a little like waiting until you're ready to have kids. It never feels like you're ready, but you know in your heart there's no better time than now. Wouldn't you agree there's no better time than now for you to ensure that your children, Lydia and Thomas, won't have to move from the home you worked so hard to provide for them in the event that you die?"

OR

"I understand that a loved one can never be replaced, but what we have proposed here for you two is a plan for $200,000 in life insurance on each of you in order to avoid having the bills pile on as a result of lost income and all the worry that comes with not having enough money to live your life. That would be awful for any member of your family, and I am sure that's the last thing you'd want to see them endure, especially during their time of grief. What do you think?"

OR

"Tom and Mary, after analyzing your situation, what is recommended for you in regard to auto liability coverage is $250,000 for bodily injury protection and $100,000 in property damage coverage. What this means to you is that if either of you or your teenage son Thomas were to be in an accident and found to be at fault, we will provide you with protection when the other driver comes after you for money for any injuries sustained up to $250,000. Our society is very sue-happy these days, and it is very common for the other driver to get an attorney and sue for exaggerated damages when you are at fault.

"The same goes for any property damage, such as vehicle repairs or replacement and other damages to someone's lawn or fence. You might consider up to $100,000 of protection. At first glance, these amounts may look like a lot, but an auto accident can easily wrack up these unexpected expenses, especially if the accident is serious. Getting this coverage through us also guarantees that we will step in and handle all the legal issues and damages on your behalf that your policy affords, thus protecting your personal assets (like savings, your kids' college funds, personal property, and investments) from being seized as part of a settlement. It will help you avoid the worry and hassle of finding legal representation if you are sued by the other party. In that light, this coverage is worth it. Do you see how this would work for you and your family?"

We may debate the effectiveness of the specific verbiage in the preceding examples given, as it is certain that someone reading this book will have better scripts to make the point. Instead, place your focus on how I use facts in support of the emotional reasons why people buy life insurance or auto insurance.

"If you want to influence, persuade, or motivate people, you have to make emotional contact with them." ~ Bert Decker, *You've Got to Be Heard to Be Believed*

Before holding sales conversations, plan out word for word what you are going to say to the customer. Get used to using emotional language, metaphors, stories, and illustrations to stimulate not only the left brain (the factual/logical side of the mind), but also the right brain (the seat of emotions and the impulse to buy).

If you want to sell well, to be different, better, and more successful than your peers, learn to speak to the right brain. Don't be a half-brained sales professional

No One Will Have Done You a Favor by Buying from You

On the surface, I am sure the above title sounds arrogant, but it isn't meant to be. Instead, it is rooted in gratefulness and in the realization that the noble profession we have chosen—the insurance and financial services profession—is one of the greatest professions conceived by the mind of man.

In a world where people toil to make an honest living and work to provide for their needs and the needs of their families, we get to do one of the better things in life and sell insurance.

What I mean by that statement is this: There are a lot of good and great things people can do for a living. There are professions and lifelong pursuits such as being a physician to the poor and underprivileged, counseling and caring for the mentally ill and those in crisis, being a nurse, a fireman, policeman, and countless other vocations which can be said to be noble in serving the common good of all mankind. These individuals, and others like them, are heroes and are to be honored for the sacrifices and risks they take on behalf of others, but these are not the only noble pursuits.

Anthony D. Cefalu

OUR PROFESSION IS A NOBLE PURSUIT. WE SERVE THE COMMON GOOD OF ALL MANKIND

For those of us who are agents, advisors, and consultants who sell insurance products and financial services can proudly say that our profession is a cool profession—albeit one so often misunderstood and unfairly maligned by the general public. Our profession is vital to industry, to our high standard of living, to innovation and invention. It is a profession that is the foundation for so many other industries and people. Take away the insurance and financial services industry, and you do damage to the entire landscape of society.

KEEPING THE PROMISES OTHER PEOPLE MAKE

We help keep the promises other people make to their loved ones and business partners. Though a loved one may die, a home may burn down, a business ambition is lost, or a car is stolen, we are there for our clients, keeping the promises they have made to their families, their friends, and their colleagues and business partners by way of insurance protection. We are the means to an end, and that end has nothing to do with what it is that we sell, but what we and what our products can do for the people we cater to.

So if we are so cool, why do people have such a low opinion of our industry and profession? Who is to blame for our poor public image? To a large degree, those of us who work in this industry are to blame for the negativity and distrust dominating public opinion. Simply put, we aren't talkative enough about the great things we do for people. Our problem is in a failure to tell our story when we should.

WE DON'T TELL OUR STORY TO ENOUGH PEOPLE ENOUGH OF THE TIME

We need to tell our story, to talk about our good deeds in restoring people and making them whole financially. We need to make sure people hear about how we've helped others avoid financial ruin or getting into a financial crucible where bankruptcy would have been the only option. We need to let people know that insurance saves the day for their friends and loved ones.

CONSIDER WHAT WE DO, AND YOU'LL UNDERSTAND WHY WE'RE COOL

That's right, we are cool. We are in a great and noble industry, and when I hear people quip about how insurance is a 'rip off' or complain about how we work to deny claims and to not pay what we promise, I let people know it's simply not true.

Why? Because I know and respect the people who make the industry so wonderful. They are good people, dedicated and hardworking individuals, and in tribute to them, I often tell the story of how insurance and the industry is one of the noblest professions around and how it can keep accidents from turning into tragedies by way of financial hardship.

CONSIDER LIFE INSURANCE & THE IMPACT A POLICY CAN HAVE ON A FAMILY'S FUTURE

For example, the loss of a loved one is devastating, to say the least. As a human being who loves people and cares for them deeply, I wish I could take the pain and grief left for the surviving family members away when someone dies, but I can't. No one can truly take away their heartache. It is what it is, and life goes on, and we can only pray and hope the future is brighter for those left behind to carry on.

But things don't always move forward as hoped. In fact, it is my observation that the loss of a loved one does one of two things to the surviving family members. It either brings a family together, making them closer than ever. Or, death tears a family apart and drives a wedge between brothers and sisters, husbands and wives, fostering resentment and bitter feelings in the aftermath of a loss.

The reasons can vary widely as to why a division among family members can occur. Nonetheless, bills piling up in the aftermath of a loved one's death dramatically increases the likelihood for strife and a rift among family and friends.

Enter the miracle of life insurance, which provides families and individuals with the liberty to deal with the pressures of losing a loved one and the associated financial pressures that follow. The agent who sells a life insurance policy today may very well be preserving the relationships of brothers, sisters, sons, daughters, mothers, and fathers for generations to come. I'll bet you never really thought of it that way before, did you? But like I said, we are cool.

I DID NOT DRINK THE KOOL-AID®

I am not an apologist for the insurance industry, nor am I someone who blindly follows along, drinking the Kool-Aid® of mindless agreement with everything we do. I also don't think they need me to argue in support of what they do, as I believe their actions and good deeds speak for themselves.

Are there bad actors in the industry, companies that have questionable business practices? Yes. What industry doesn't have its share of problem children? But those are few in number, and they do get policed. Heightened vigilance in the industry to make sure consumers are treated fairly and right is something I am fully in support of in order to avoid and stop abuses and other misconduct by insurance companies.

DON'T GUSH ALL OVER WHEN PEOPLE BUY FROM YOU, IF YOU KNOW WHAT I MEAN

Bottom line, when someone buys from you, be grateful that they chose you as their trusted advisor, their insurance agent, who is responsible for making sure they are protected for what they need and want. Gratitude is a good thing, an appropriate reaction toward a customer who selects you and trusts you to be their agent, particularly since there are so many agent choices out there today.

What isn't appropriate is the notion of gratefulness born out of a sense of unworthiness or favor. It is not healthy to think of yourself as lucky or fortunate to have had someone actually do business with you, as if the customer has better choices than you for an agent. That's nonsense! You are the best thing going!

YOU ARE THE BETTER CHOICE

In my opinion; some agents (particularly new ones) do feel a bit of the unhealthy gratitude I just mentioned. The quicker that kind of thinking is dispensed with, the better for you as a professional.

Bottom line: No one will have ever done you a favor by buying from you. It is you who has done them a favor by seeking them out as a prospect, planning a sales conversation that is persuasive and compelling, monitoring their needs, and meeting with them periodically to review their situation and adjust their individualized insurance plan so it is current and relevant for what they want and need.

That's a lot of work, energy, concern, and dedication to invest in a client, and that's exactly why no one will have ever done you a favor by buying from you. We earn our living by making sure other's lives are secure, and for that reason, our clients should be thanking us for doing the worrying for them so they don't have to. No one will ever have done you a favor by buying from you; you are the one doing the favor!

The Key to an Effective Close is a Powerful Opening

The opening stage of a sales conversation is fundamentally critical to the success or failure in closing a sale. It is during these precious initial moments of meeting a customer for the first time that value is either perceived or not perceived.

As the old cliché goes, you never get a second chance at making a good first impression. It is during the opening phase, or first impression stage, when meeting someone that they form opinions of you, the sales professional. Those opinions define for the individual whether or not you bring value to them and whether or not they can and will do business with you. Thus, a powerful opening to the sales conversation that creates a positive first impression for the customer about you can determine your success or failure.

An example of an opening that presumes an agency situation and a scenario where the customer is interested in buying auto and homeowners' insurance will be presented. The sales conversation is led by a fully licensed and trained agency staff team member, not the agent-owner.

Please note that many of the points made here are not unique to the insurance and financial services industry per se, but are transferable to other sales situations and disciplines as well.

Anthony D. Cefalu

Additional comments beyond the scripting of an opening will be provided for your benefit.

Finally, the point should be clear that this is an example and not the definitive way to open a sales conversation. It is a starting point for you to consider when formulating your own strategy, style, and language. The final version of your opening may look completely different.

Simply note that when you do structure an opening of your own, make sure it is a reproducible and systematic process; it should contain all the elements of who you are, what you do, what the agency or business is about that you work for, and—most importantly—what benefit you bring to all those who do business with you.

"Hi, Bill. I'm Jerry Smith. Thank you for coming in today and taking time out of your busy schedule to meet with me about your auto and homeowners' needs. That's commendable on your part, knowing how important these matters can be for you and your family. Besides, it's always a pleasure for me to have the opportunity to meet with new people like yourself and build new friendships and relationships as a result."

This stage is critical. Begin developing some rapport with the customer. Get into their world and ask them what we call 'F.O.R.C.E. questions': about their family ("Do you have any children?"), occupation ("What do you do for a living?"), recreational hobbies ("Do you enjoy the outdoors?"), community issues ("Are you originally from this area?"), and/or education ("Where did you go to school?"). These are excellent conversation starters.

TO BE INTERESTED IS INTERESTING

These are subjects that appeal to people. They are easy to recall and address and do not create any undue stress for the customer to have to think about and answer. Additionally, asking questions about the customer is to ask questions about their favorite subject,

Pull Your Nose Up

themselves! Be interested in your customers and in turn they will find you just as interesting.

BEING 'PSYCHO' CAN BE A GOOD THING

Anytime you offer or give something to the customer, the psychological effect of reciprocity (which we've already discussed) is put into play. In brief, this is a human response that says, "You get what you give." In other words, there is a deep-seated desire in the great majority of people to respond in kind whenever something is given or offered.

A gift or giveaway of any kind subtly obligates the customer to give back something in return or respond back, either by opening up to you in the sales conversation, or better yet, by buying from you. Either way, hospitality is always part of the recipe when meeting customers. It is simply the right way to behave with people anyway.

LISTEN PEOPLE INTO BUYING

Also, make sure the customer is given your full attention. Minimize distractions or interruptions on the part of the phone or colleagues in the office. Don't be guilty of letting your eyes wonder off into space or, worse yet, out the window to see what is going on outside. Customers will sense your distraction and begin to build negative feelings toward you. Make them feel important like they desire; focus your eyes and your attention on them at all times.

YOUR OFFICE ENVIRONMENT CAN BE INVITING OR THREATENING TO A CUSTOMER

Evaluate your work space. Is it conducive to sales conversations? Can you have open, candid conversations with customers without being overheard by other office colleagues or customers in the waiting area? Privacy is important in the business you are in.

Anthony D. Cefalu

THE BODY CAN SPEAK LOUDER THAN WORDS

Look for the smile, the open body language, the relaxation of the shoulders. These are signs of mental momentum in the sales process, indicating that the customer is mentally relaxing and increasingly at ease with you, more apt to listen to you attentively and positively. These are your cues for you to move forward in the sales conversation.

"Before we get started, I'd like to take a minute to introduce myself and talk about my role here in the agency and how it relates to you as a potential client. I'd also like to tell you a little about our agency and how we work and about our company [You can get name specific here] *and what it means to our clients to have us in their court. How does that sound?* [Pause] *Great.*

"Well, to begin with, I've been with Company X for over eight years now, working with several different agents to gain the experience and expertise our customers look for and appreciate in an agency. The first couple of years, I began as an assistant to the agency office manager, helping families like yours with auto and homeowners' claims and servicing any of their other insurance needs. I'm now fully licensed by the State in property and casualty insurance, which is auto and homeowners' insurance, and I was recently appointed by Tom as the agency expert for all our customers' needs in the auto and homeowners' insurance arena."

In this segment, don't be shy. Position yourself as the expert when it is true. Some people feel uncomfortable about characterizing themselves as experts or professionals. For those who aren't experts and professionals, I can understand the reluctance, but for those of you who have the experience, the training, and the qualifications to call yourself an expert, do so.

DON'T SELL YOURSELF SHORT

If you do not mention your abilities and attributes, you are literally selling yourself short with the customer and missing out on the

Pull Your Nose Up

opportunity to create value in their mind. If you're worth it, tell them as professionally and humbly as you can.

"What that means is, I'll be your personal resource for any questions, concerns, or needs you may have when it comes to auto and homeowners' insurance. In fact, that's what's so unique about our office. Each of us is an expert in a particular area such as life, health, financial services and investments, banking, and—in my case—auto and homeowners' insurance. That allows us to concentrate all our efforts on being your expert resource in each respective area. It's like having your own personal consultant just a phone call away.

"Our clients just love knowing that we're here for them whenever they need us. We'd work the same way for you if you were to make us your insurance agent of choice as well. Whether it's an auto accident you've been involved in, a homeowners' claim for theft or fire, the purchase of a new car, or simply a billing question, I'm here for you, ready to help you personally, 24/7, for convenient, quick service without the fear and frustration that comes with 1-800 number insurance companies. We believe in personally being there for you. That's our commitment to you—to take care of those things so you don't have to worry about them.

"Our agency office hours are from nine to five p.m. Monday through Friday and nine to noon on Saturdays. If that doesn't fit into your schedule, we're always available to meet with you at your convenience by appointment. Just give us a call, and we'll be there for you. How does that sound?

"We do have twenty-four-hour service through our office number in case you need to reach us in the middle of the night, when many accidents or problems occur. Also, Tom's home phone number is listed in the phone book, so you can contact him any time you may have an emergency.

"We're a full-service office. That is, you can pay your bill here, bank here, get a car loan and invest your money here. You can even get a

cup of coffee here if you like! We take care of all those things for you, as well as your insurance needs—all in one convenient place.

"Here's a brochure that speaks to the variety of services we offer to you and your family. And by the way, if what we talk about today ever comes up in conversation with a friend, coworker, or family member, I'd appreciate your help in telling them about what we do for people. In fact, that's how most of our clients come to meet us and do business with us—through the recommendation of one of our satisfied customers. We're like a family here, and we work to make sure you, your loved ones, and your friends are fully protected against the unexpected.

"We're here for you when you need us, whatever you need. That's our commitment to each of our clients, which is why I stated earlier that we are a rather unique office." Wouldn't you agree?

"And lastly, our customers can rely on Company X's strength and leadership in the industry. That's over $XX million dollars of stability for our XX million policyholders nationwide, assuring them we'll be there for them when they need us. Our agency itself insures over 3,000 families in the Atlanta area alone—that's 3,000 families just like yours who rely on us and trust us to make sure they are fully protected with their auto, homeowners', life, and health insurance needs. They also entrust us with their financial needs through investments and banking services that we offer. We stand by our promise to protect you and pay claims. Everyone from the towing company to the body shop knows us because of our reputation and prominence in the industry, so things can move smoothly for you when something happens. We're big enough to pay our claims and local enough to be right here for you when you need us."

Notice the three elements in the previous segment: you (the agent), the agency, and the company. Notice also how each fact or feature mentioned about each element is subsequently translated into a benefit statement pointing to *what it all means* to the customer.

Anytime a sales professional mentions a fact or feature about someone or something, it must be converted into language that resonates positively with the customer. One simple way to accomplish this task is to use the bridging phrase, "What this means to you is…"

"With that in mind, we are meeting to discuss your auto and homeowners' insurance. As you well know, auto and homeowners' is more than just fixing a dent in a car or replacing blown-off shingles. It's also about protecting your family assets and the family money you have worked so hard to accumulate over your lifetime. In order for me to gain an understanding of your current situation and what you are looking for in terms of coverage, I need to ask you a few questions. How does that sound? [Pause] Great."

The great folly of most sales professionals is to state facts about themselves and their business without relating it to the benefits the customer will realize and appreciate. That kind of company- or product-centered talk has nothing to do with the customer and everything to do with the salesperson and the company they represent.

CUSTOMERS DO NOT RESPOND WELL TO THAT TYPE OF CONVERSATION

People Want to Feel Special. They Want to Talk About What Is Important to Them, Not What Is Important to You.

Differentiate yourself from the competition and begin to talk in customer-centered sales language. It begins the moment you first meet them with the opening to the sales conversation.

During that time, tell customers what you mean to them, what your agency or business means for them, and what you can do to meet their needs.

They don't care about anything else when buying, so give them what they want…right from the start.

Principles Endure, and Methodologies Vary

In the insurance and financial services industry, evaluating the effectiveness of a marketing plan can sometimes be a difficult venture. As a manager, I was often called upon by agents to assess whether or not a particular marketing plan was strong and made sense for the agent it was designed to help.

The following are some basic principles that can be used to gauge the effectiveness of a particular marketing plan in a very short time. A solid plan will adhere to the following:

1. **Does it incorporate *systematic processes* for marketing?** That is, are those marketing process spelled out specifically and codified into a document that others can use and execute from if needed? Have you written down each step necessary in implementing the systematic marketing process?

2. **Does each marketing process truly focus on marketing?** Simply said, marketing consists of all those things we do to get people in front of us. It does contain an element of retention, meaning that marketing is about getting customers, but it also has to do with keeping customers. In placing a priority on getting customers, each process employed in a marketing plan has to stand the *Golden Rule Test*. This rule states that if what you are doing does not have a marketing end to it in getting people in front of you, you must ask yourself, "Why am I doing it?" Being busy

doesn't mean busy about the right things. Evaluate your processes; their worth is directly related to their marketing usefulness.

3. **Does each marketing process target growth opportunities?** It's a simple question of line of sight. Are your 'marketing eyes' focused on the right target so you will get results you need?

4. **Does the marketing process lend itself to repetitive action?** If your marketing process is to be effective in the long term, it must be reproducible as a habit for marketing.

5. **Does the marketing plan take a balanced approach of marketing both internally and externally?** Are you mining the agency base for new cross-selling opportunities as well as external, new customer business? A focus weighted too heavily in either direction represents a situation that is not optimized for steady, solid agency growth.

6. **Does the marketing plan incorporate both passive (reactive) and active (proactive) processes for driving customers to your sales portals?** Too often, marketing plans incorporate an inordinate amount of passive processes, ignoring the value of active processes that require the agency to reach out to potential customers.

7. **Does your marketing plan pass the *Return on Investment* (ROI) test?** Each marketing activity should be measured for its ROI. If the ROI isn't a positive one (i.e., bringing in more money to the agency than what it costs to implement), it should be abandoned.

Pull Your Nose Up

> 1. Marketing is composed of systematic processes.
> 2. Marketing must focus on getting people in front of you.
> 3. Marketing must target growth opportunities.
> 4. Marketing must be a habit (lending itself to repetitive processes).
> 5. Marketing must be balanced in its approach to mine internal customers and seek external prospects simultaneously.
> 6. Marketing utilizes both passive(reactive) and active processes (reaching out to new customers).
> 7. Marketing must produce a positive return on investment.

Marketing is simple, but the execution of marketing is a different story. It tends to be a tough undertaking for some people to stick to a plan and execute on processes regularly and systematically.

Before you execute on your plan, place it under the microscope of these seven principles. In the end, you'll be more productive and more confident about the activities you are undertaking within your agency.

When Great Customer Service Can Kill Your Business

Agents sometimes defer to service work over sales and dedicated marketing work in their daily business operations and small businesses. Why? Because service work is easier than sales and marketing work most of the time.

The premise for focusing on extraordinary customer service as an owner is that it helps with retention of the current clientele in an economic environment where every retained policyholder represents a precious income stream into the agency operation.

At first, the logic of providing extraordinary customer service rings true to the ears of the listener and makes sense when spoken by anyone who runs a small business, especially when everyone else is saying the same thing. But in reality, a focus that emphasizes extraordinary customer service as the single best means to achieving success and growth in the marketplace is a business philosophy destined for failure.

It is a reality of human nature to fall prey to the temptation of taking the path of least resistance when it comes to accomplishing certain things in life. Unfortunately, the path of least resistance all too often represents outcomes that are less than favorable for the agency-owner.

Therefore, when we excuse away the proactive activities associated with aggressively capturing market share and creating customers for the passive activity of providing 'unsurpassed customer service', we make a grave mistake in defining what exactly it is that differentiates us in the marketplace and sets us apart from our competitors.

Please understand, I am not discounting the value of good customer service. What I am critical of is the unreasonable focus and almost arrogant notion that agent-owners and staff members assume with their personal charge and pursuit of providing superior customer service over the noble effort of selling to people the products they so desperately need from us.

Selling activities are proactive; they require movement and initiative in order to be successful. Selling represents risk. It involves resistance and work and planning. It requires the investment of time, ideas, effort, money, intellectual energy, and emotional investment. It can be physically stressful as well. In essence, selling represents uncertainty.

CUSTOMER SERVICE IS TOUGH. MARKETING AND SELLING IS TOUGHER.

Great customer service can kill your business…

…When you prefer to please rather than persuade someone.
…When you choose being busy over being productive.
…When you think service is more important than securing someone's lifestyle and dreams
…When you would rather react to circumstances instead of reach out to people.
…When you live under the false premise that customer service is the best way to generate future sales into the agency

Are you killing your business with customer service? Are you too busy being the good guy, the good agent or staff team member who goes beyond the norm when taking care of policyholder problems, questions, or concerns?

Pull Your Nose Up

If so, it's time to shift your agency into a sales organization. In sales, nice guys really do finish last!

Claim Day is Game Day

"There is one thing that is common to every individual, relationship, team, family, organization, nation, economy, and civilization throughout the world—one thing which, if removed, will destroy the most powerful government, the most successful business . . . On the other hand, if developed and leveraged, that one thing has the potential to create unparalleled success and prosperity in every dimension of life. Yet it is the least understood, most neglected, and most underestimated possibility of our time. That one thing is trust."
~ Stephen R. Covey, The Speed of Trust

What is your strategy for handling claims? What process do you have in place for handling customers, who at the time of a claim, are often stressed and at a high emotional pique?

If sales is about a relationship between the agent and the customer, what better opportunity is there to earn and solidify that relationship than at the time of a claim?

Customers are emotional creatures. Logic does factor into the decision-making and buying process, but it is our feelings, our emotions that rule the day when the two are juxtaposed.

Anthony D. Cefalu

TRUST IS A PRECIOUS COMMODITY OF THE SUCCESSFUL BUSINESS PERSON

Our customers trust us to keep our promise of being there for them in their time of need. Trust is that emotional factor that says, "I have confidence in you and in what you say."

Trust is the promise kept, the pledge made real, the feeling you have in a relationship that dispels any notions of suspicion and worry that is so common to other relationships people have in life. Insurance agents, in particular, are in the trust business.

WITHOUT TRUST, THE ENTIRE INSURANCE INDUSTRY IS IRRELEVANT

Customers want to trust us. They want to feel assured that if the day ever comes when a claim has to be made, they can trust that everyone—agent, claim representative, and company—will keep their promise to pay the claim. That is what the customer expects.

From a business standpoint, why not devise a claims strategy that seizes upon the most opportune moment an agent has to showcase their worth, value, and trustworthiness to serve the customer?

"Transcendent values like trust and integrity literally translate into revenue, profits and prosperity." ~ Patricia Aburdene, Megatrends

A TWO-PRONGED APPROACH: THE SALES PROFESSIONAL AS GUIDE AND GUARDIAN

As *guide*, you can walk the customer through the stages of the claims process, allaying their fears and concerns; dispelling any myths or mysteries about what they can expect; while, in turn, strengthening the agent-customer relationship.

Claim time is game time for the agent—an opportunity to showcase

Pull Your Nose Up

who you, the agent, really are for the customer: a trusted advisor and competent resource in their time of need and worry.

But isn't that what claim representatives are supposed to do? Don't they settle the claim and help keep the promises we make to our customers? Yes, companies do have competent professionals trained specifically to assist customers in settling their claims. I am not suggesting that agents circumvent the claim representative and the entire claims process. What I am suggesting is that agents 'enhance' the claims experience by insinuating themselves into the process in order to gain positive emotional points toward customer trust, loyalty, and future sales.

CLAIM TIME IS ONE OF THE BEST TIMES TO PROVE YOU ARE NOT LIKE THE COMPETITION

Be different. Be trustworthy. It solidifies relationships, engenders customer loyalty, and leads to future profits and referrals. It shows you are not like the other insurance companies out there; you are better, extraordinary.

"Technique and technology are important, but adding trust is the issue of the decade." ~ Tom Peters, Author and Business Expert

In the role of *guardian*, the agent's duty is to review and re-underwrite the claim when necessary and to respond appropriately based on the customer's prior claim activity. Claims frequency and severity to the insurance professional are the critical components to business profits.

It may be that as guardian, you will meet with the customer to specifically advise them of their situation and coverage risks based on their claims activity or changing household dynamics. When this is done in a kind and thoughtful manner, the customer will appreciate the discussion and concerns you may have for their wellbeing and may actually take action on your recommendations.

Anthony D. Cefalu

The result of being a guardian is that you will be perceived as more than just a salesperson. You will be a friend, a resource, a trusted advisor, and a guardian of your customer's best interest, as well as that of the agency and its profitability.

A SUGGESTED ROADMAP FOR CLAIMS HANDLING

I. When the claim is filed…

A. Explain the claims process to the customer. Script out and rehearse what you will say to ensure that you are consistent and uniform in what is said to customers every time a claim is reported to the agency. Be their guide. Explaining what to expect and who will be calling them from claims to assist them through the details of the process is an effective way to reduce any fear or concerns on the part of the customer. They will appreciate you caring enough to take the time to explain it all to them.

B. Reassure the customer on an emotional level that they are not alone in this process and that everything will be properly handled. Consider using *emotionally based* terminology such as: "I understand how you feel. We are a phone call away. We're here for you if you have any questions or concerns, Our claims personnel will help you. Call anytime. We're here to help. I'm so glad you are alright."

As insurance professionals, our day-to-day exposure to insurance matters can sometimes remove us from the emotional impact a claim has on a customer. Don't forget to be empathetic and appropriately consoling to customers when they experience a loss. It can only strengthen the business relationship you already have with them.

If you become good at being a guide and guardian to your customers, you will allay their fears, remind them of the reason why they bought from you in the first place, and it will showcase the added value they have in you as their insurance agent. The

Pull Your Nose Up

result is you will have a created a customer for life… assuming you want to keep them!

C. Assist your customers in securing a rental car or any other issue related to the claim. As a reminder, I am not suggesting you handle the claim. That's what claim representatives do for us. I am simply recommending a few simple measures that can be taken initially by the agent which can have a profound impact on customer loyalty and overall business success in the future.

D. Follow up with the customer. Establish an in-office claims handling process that allows you to follow up by phone, letter, or even email (preferably a phone conversation) to check on the status of the claim and to reinforce in the customer's mind that you care about them.

E. Review the household following a claim when appropriate; that is what being a guardian means. Claim time is a marketing opportunity for the agent. Anytime you have a reason to meet or a reason to speak to someone, it is a marketing opportunity.

When meeting with a customer who is going through a claim or has just concluded one, take the opportunity to review with them those things that may be affecting the frequency or severity of claims in their household.

For example:

1. Why are they having the claim frequency or severity they are experiencing?

2. Is something going on within the household that would be triggering these issues for your customer? (e.g. undisclosed driver or unknown youthful driver in the household, a household business venture)

3. What options are available to the customer to reduce the likelihood of future claims? (e.g. raising deductibles, adding

coverage, adopting certain measures to mitigate possible future losses)

4. How can we help assist the customer from jeopardizing their continued eligibility for insurance coverage?

EXAMPLE PHONE WORD TRACK TO FOLLOW UP WITH A CLAIM:

"Hi, Tom. This is Eric from the XYZ Insurance Agency here in Worcester. The reason I'm calling is that we were reviewing your file and realized we hadn't had the opportunity to meet with you since your automobile accident back in September.

"There's no better time to be sure your family is properly protected than after a claim is made. Oftentimes, a quick review of a family's entire insurance and financial situation reveals either a way to save money or a gap exposing their family to unnecessary risk.

"My other clients really appreciate the peace of mind that comes in taking fifteen minutes to review their situation in order to make sure their family is safe and protected in case another claim has to be made. I am sure you will as well.

"I just called to see when would be the best time for us to get together...The next available appointment I have is...Will that work for you?"

Claim Day is truly game day for the agent. Score a win for yourself by devising a specific strategy as guide to your customers and guardian of their interests and your own profitability as a small business owner.

Paralyzed by Perfection

"There is no level of success for which we can wade into shore." ~ Peter Block, The Answer to How is Yes

Oftentimes, when talking with a sales professional who is having difficulty selling a particular line of insurance or financial products, I'm told the following is the root of the problem: "I'm just not comfortable discussing the product with customers. Until I fully understand how the product works, I can't sell it."

Thus, presumably the solution to slumping sales results or reluctance to sell a product at all is the need for additional training. With more study, more dissection of the product details, successful sales and marketing results will follow, according to those who adopt such a philosophy.

"The process of achievement comes through repeated failures and the constant struggle to climb to a higher level." ~ John Maxwell, Attitude 101

On its surface, the argument for more product training sounds reasonable, but in reality, the problem of not selling isn't for lack of good product training or knowledge; rather, the problem behind not selling a product line oftentimes lies in a lack of doing rather than a lack of knowing.

Anthony D. Cefalu

KNOWLEDGE DOES NOT PRECEDE DOING. DOING PRECEDES KNOWLEDGE.

"Action is the real measure of intelligence." ~ Napoleon Hill

John C. Maxwell, author, teacher, and expert on leadership and motivation writes an account in his book, *Attitude 101: What Every Leader Needs to Know*, in which an art teacher of ceramics made an interesting discovery about how people think and behave and the outcomes they realize as a result.

Specifically, this ceramics teacher announced to his students that there would be two grading systems for the class: One group of students would be graded strictly on the quality of the clay pot they produced for the grading period; and the other group of students would be graded strictly on the quantity of clay pots they produced in the same grading period. For the second group, those with fifty pounds of clay pots would receive an A, those with forty pounds a B, and so on.

At the end of the grading period, a "curious fact emerged" among the two competing groups, according to Maxwell. Those pots of the highest quality actually came from the group who was being graded solely on quantity. Why? While those who were in the quality group anguished and pained over every minute detail of their one pot, the quantity group was improving on their skills and abilities with each new clay pot they undertook.

THERE IS NOT A MORE PERFECT TIME TO DO SOMETHING THAN NOW

Rather than immersing themselves in the details of a quality product, the quantity group worked at creating and perfecting with each attempt and act to create. The result of their actions was a clay pot of superior quality.

"Do not wait; the time will never be 'just right'. Start where you stand;

Pull Your Nose Up

and work with whatever tools you may have at your command, and better tools will be found as you go along." ~ Napoleon Hill

THE LESSON FOR ALL SALES PROFESSIONALS

Do not be paralyzed by the thought of having to be perfect right at the start as an agent, consultant, or financial adviser. Don't use the excuse of needing more product training as the reason you are not selling a particular product or service.

Only when a person refuses to be paralyzed with the notion that complete and flawless product knowledge is necessary in order to be able to sell well can that person actually begin to sell well.

Just do the work of selling, and quality will follow as a result.

Be Deliberately Successful

"We rule men with words." ~ *Napoleon*

"The difference between the right word and the almost right word is the difference between lightning and a lightning bug." ~ Mark Twain

AD-LIBBING IS FOR AMATEURS

The above quotes are from two notable men in history, and as such, it is understood that what a person says and how it is said can be the defining difference between success and failure in almost any endeavor.

Understanding the power of words and being able to harness that power to persuade others effectively is a distinguishing talent of superstar agents and salespeople.

Superstar agents understand that the finest product or service in the world will not sell itself. It takes a carefully crafted, artfully delivered construct of words to communicate effectively with people in order to be understood and persuasive at the same time. In other words…

THE SALESPERSON WITH THE BEST WORDS WINS

As a salesperson, we call these carefully selected words a 'sales script'. To some, the very thought of using a script is tantamount to professional sacrilege, but to the wise and those who wish to elevate their sales results above being average, scripts—good scripts, that is—are an indispensable means to that end.

The difference between a great career and an average career can be seen in whether one is deliberate in being successful and another person is random.

RANDOM ACTS OF SUCCESS? IS THAT EVEN POSSIBLE?

Success doesn't just happen; it is the confluence of a deliberate plan to be successful meeting with its deliberate execution. I will concede that some people have achieved success randomly or accidentally, but that would be the exception to what I commonly see required of success—to be deliberate and thoughtful in planning to be successful.

Yes, random acts of success have been known to happen, but choosing the random philosophy for one's career is going to be a regrettable wait for practically anyone who works and lives that way. I choose not to wait for life and success to just happen to me. Instead, I try to make it happen as best as I can.

SCRIPTING: A HABIT OF MANY SUCCESSFUL PEOPLE

Scripting harnesses the power of organized information. It eliminates the awkwardness and confusion present in many sales conversations, thus promoting an increased likelihood of your listeners to understand what it is you are saying. It also makes adopting your ideas and plans much more likely than with an unscripted, unplanned discussion or presentation.

Additionally, it creates a relaxed atmosphere for both sales professional and prospect. One of the more frustrating and tense aspects of the sales profession is the inability or uncertainty by many sales professionals to find the right words to say to people in a given situation. Scripting eliminates that tension and provides everyone with a better environment to meet and talk.

Pull Your Nose Up

THE WILL TO WIN IS NOT AS IMPORTANT AS THE WILL TO PLAN TO WIN

Every serious sales professional should have a script book in order to keep record of effective word tracks. These books are not only useful in building one's individual communication skill level, but they also serve as excellent training guides whenever new staff is hired into the agency.

SCRIPT BOOK: A RECOMMENDED WAY TO ORGANIZE SCRIPTS FOR FUTURE REFERENCE

Get a three-ring binder and place dividers in it to separate your scripts into categories similar to the following:

SALES

1. Auto Sales Conversation
2. Homeowners' Sales Conversation
3. Life Sales Conversation
4. Commercial/Small Business Sales Conversation
5. Investment Sales Conversation (Variable Products, Fixed Products)
6. Props/Proofs & Other Media Sources to be Used at the Point of Sale
    a. Persuasive Facts and Figures
    b. Current News Articles/Magazines Articles
    c. Sales Conversation Tools/Visuals/Graphics/Other Produced Sales Discussion Platforms Used at the Point of Sale

MARKETING

1. Other Scripts
    a. X-date Phone Script
    b. Appointment Follow-Up Phone Script
    c. Premium/Price Change Phone Script
    d. Claims Handling Phone Script

e. Review/Insurance Check-Up Phone Script
f. Confirm the Appointment Phone Script
g. Competitive Auto/Homeowners Quote Phone Script
h. Follow-Up/Re-quote Phone Script
i. Complaint Handling Phone Script
j. Thank You for Your Business/Birthday/Congratulations Phone Script
k. Auto/No Home Phone Script
l. Home/No Auto Phone Script
m. Multi-line or Life Phone Script
n. No Automatic Bank Withdrawal to Pay Premium Phone Script
o. Service + 1 Phone Script or Walk-in Script
p. I Just Want a Quote Phone Script
q. Up Front Commercial Script/or Introduction Script
r. Referral Script

2. Objections & Concerns Scripts
   a. No Need
   b. No Money
   c. No Time
   d. No Interest

3. Processes (Who, When, Where, How, What): Step-by-Step Plan of How a Particular Marketing Process will be Executed, When it Will be Executed, What will be said and Who will implement it.
   a. External/new business marketing
      (1.) X-dating for Auto Competitive Quotes
      (2.) Call-in/Walk-in quotes
      (3.) Referral System
      (4.) Community & Civic Events/Church, Clubs, Membership to Organizations, Events
      (5.) Centers of Influence (e.g. apartment complexes, realtors, small businesses)
      (6.) Telemarketing Systems
      (7.) Friends/Family/Acquaintances
   b. Internal/Retention & Cross Selling Processes (Who, What, Where, When, How)

(1.) New Client Follow-Up System
(2.) Price Increase Follow-Up System
(3.) Claims Handling System
(4.) Review/Insurance Check-Up System
(5.) Small Business/Commercial Marketing System
(6.) Re-quote/Follow-Up System
(7.) Motorcycle/Bike Night System
(8.) Birthday Card/Thank You System
(9.) Auto Discussion-Pivot to Life Discussion System

It may initially appear that putting together a script book is unnecessary work, but it isn't. Think of it this way: If we require of doctors and airplane pilots and lawyers, for example, to be professionals who know their craft inside and out by way of study, memorization, and deliberate practice, why should we require any less of ourselves?

Also, if we desire to be taken seriously and to earn the privilege of being called a *sales professional*, we need to take up responsibilities akin to what it takes to earn that title.

SCRIPTING IS HARNESSING THE POWER OF WORDS

Scripting is the means by which insurance agents can earn the title of 'professional, expert, advisor and trusted consultant'. It is the work, duty, and responsibility of insurance sales professional to be able to effectively communicate with individuals as powerfully as possible in order to persuade them to do those things they need to do for themselves—like buy insurance.

Be deliberately successful!

Ideas Are a Dime a Dozen, But Their Execution is Priceless

Quite often, it appears as if we are in search of a secret formula that will get the phone ringing and bring customers into the agency asking to buy from us.

Companies sponsor seminars, showcase the big hitters in sales production at conventions, host marketing and sales discussion groups, and publish 'best practices' for their sales force, all in the hopes of discovering some hidden treasure of success for their agents to use in order to increase production.

For a nominal fee of 'only $600' or some other ridiculous price, agents willingly line up with wallets open to sign up for the latest new book or speaker who will share with them the veiled secrets to sales success thought reserved only for a privileged elite class of professionals.

I have heard it said, "Instead of learning the tricks of the trade, why not just learn the trade?" This is sound advice for all of us, sales professionals and non-sales professionals alike.

LEARNING SHOULD LEAD TO ACTION. SIMPLY KNOWING MEANS NOTHING.

"Action is eloquence." ~ *William Shakespeare*

Anthony D. Cefalu

There is no substitute for the sales professional who gets it done in terms of results and sales growth and profits. Getting it done reigns supreme over the sales professional with ChFC, CLU, FLMI, AIC, CFP, and any other designation the insurance and financial services industry can envision.

Please do not misunderstand me. Professional designations are important. They lend a lot of credibility to the competency of an insurance and financial services professional. Yet, if the knowledge gained in these courses is not applied to everyday life as a professional, they mean absolutely nothing beyond proof of an individual's ability to pass a test.

DON'T CONFUSE CLASSROOM ATTENDANCE AND BOOK LEARNING WITH ACCOMPLISHMENT AND RESULTS.

One is simply the means to accomplishing the other, if put in proper perspective. I have known people who are involved in all kinds of activities, attending sales seminars put on by marquis-named sales experts who hold every designation imaginable, yet they fail to link learning to results.

I believe in being a lifelong learner of the sales profession and the insurance industry. I am one of the biggest advocates of personal development and growth, particularly through the many opportunities our industry provides for its workers. What I do not advocate is knowledge for knowledge's sake. For me, the proof of real genius is in the application of what we know and have learned to the benefit of customers and the industry.

"I can't spare this man; he fights." ~ Abraham Lincoln on Ulysses S. Grant

One of the most frustrating things facing President Abraham Lincoln was the failure of his generals to execute on the battlefield. As brilliant and learned as they were, their weakness was in failing to place their best efforts into how to execute those battle plan strategies and ideas on the field in order to defeat the enemy.

Pull Your Nose Up

Of the military leaders President Lincoln could have chosen to lead Union forces, he selected the unpolished, but accomplished and results-driven Ulysses S. Grant over other learned and sophisticated generals of the time. Why? Because Grant linked knowing with doing. The man was a genius.

I know for many sales managers and agents managing their sales teams, this frustration is all too familiar. Yes, ideas are precious; they are generated oftentimes out of adversity or the need to overcome some difficult obstacle. Also, they are not to be taken lightly when conceived and envisioned.

BUT, IDEAS ARE A DIME A DOZEN IF NOT EXECUTED.

Do not put your best effort in coming up with or co-opting the next big sales or marketing idea. Put your best effort on *the execution* of those ideas you already know to be effective and successful.

The real magic bullet solution to most sales problems and slumps is the simple need for execution on those processes you already know to be effective in bringing customers to your place of business.

ACT, DO, EXECUTE.

Examine your in-book and out-of-book customer base and marketing strategies. Write down the two to three strategies you know to be successful when executed. Be careful not to overburden yourself with too many strategies. Simply choose the top two or three that work. Once that is done, work them. Execute! Invest your time and energies into making something happen.

While others continue to wrack their brains and search the endless horizon for sales ideas and strategies, you'll discover the true secret to success: execution.

In regard to those circumstances that you can control, stop the excuses that are so common to other sales professionals who are not growing or experiencing increased customer defection. Don't delay! The time for action and execution is now.

Don't waste your time thinking of reasons why you aren't doing anything or growing. Don't bother searching for the answers to business success, because you already know them; they have been presented to you countless times through training, experience, books, colleagues, and observation.

Don't think me insensitive or out of touch when I challenge you in this manner. I do understand that business ventures vary, that they are not the same, and that no two markets or their demographics are identical. Yes, I do understand many variables come into play in order to drive the success so many of us dream about.

What I am challenging you, however, to do is to reflect on your efforts, consider your circumstances, and look at them through the prism of honest self-evaluation. This takes courage, and I applaud anyone who makes an honest assessment of their business efforts and outcomes.

In those instances where you have a measure of control to act, do, and execute on a process or idea, I say, "Just do it!" The choice is yours. If not for any other reason, "Do it for you." You will be glad you did.

Fail Your Failures Fast & Other Talent Acquisition & Management Principles

Some of the biggest challenges facing the small business owner or agent-owner is *hiring* competent talent and *training* them to do the job well.

Talent acquisition is one of the most difficult processes for an agent-owner to undertake for a number of reasons, not the least of which is the time and money invested in recruiting, interviewing, and managing a new employee in order for them to bring in a positive return on your overall investment.

Acquiring the right staff for the right position at the right time can be the difference between continued profitability and viability as a presence in the marketplace and a slow, financial death. As the old sports cliché goes, "You can't win championships without good players, but you can lose championships with good players." In other words, staffing issues for the agent-owner exist in two distinct realms: the realm of recruiting good talent (acquisition), and the realm of managing good talent (performance).

The successful agent-owner has to learn to operate in both spaces in order to thrive or survive in today's hyper-competitive marketplace. It is the difference between hiring revenue-generating talent and expense item talent.

Anthony D. Cefalu

Talent Acquisition & Development Hierarchy

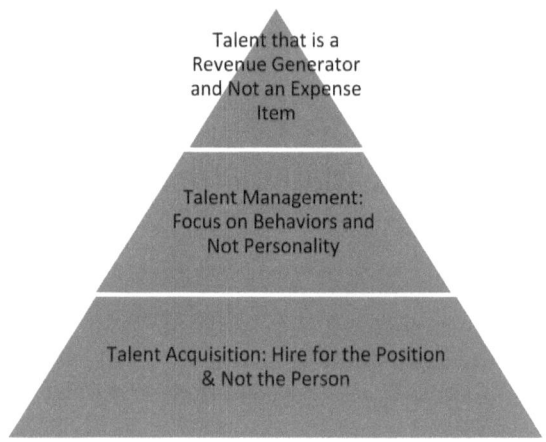

TALENT ACQUISITION & DEVELOPMENT HIERARCHY

The following principles regarding talent acquisition and assessing the hired individual for continued employment purposes and improved job performance is from a high-level perspective. I leave it to you to decide on the details of how you can execute on these principles and develop an effective agency employee and team.

1. HAVE A STRUCTURED RECRUITEMENT PROCESS. Develop a structured, written, formal recruiting process that can be sustained indefinitely. The most effective recruiting is the kind that is ongoing, whether talent is needed at the time or not. It is better to recognize talent and keep track of it in a scouting book when you don't need to currently hire anyone. Keep resumes on file for future hiring needs so that when the time comes to hire someone, you're not hurried or desperate to find someone to interview and hire. An effective recruiting process will include the following tools:
   a. A written job description

Pull Your Nose Up

    b. Recruiting letters and phone word tracks
    c. A staff handbook
    d. A phone screening questionnaire
    e. A structured interview form for the face-to-face interview
    f. A reputable skills assessment test
    g. An offer letter and rejection letter template.

Note: I am aware of the various opinions on skills assessments for recruiting purposes. In my opinion, it is not wise to hire an associate without first having them take some kind of objective skills assessment designed to measure their sales, marketing, or management acumen, depending upon the position needing filled. For the money, these assessments are worth it. The science behind many such assessments is very good in gauging an individual's prospective fitness for a given employment position. I do not consider such assessments the definitive measure of an individual's fitness for hire. But I do use them as one of several key measures in my final decision on whether to hire or not to hire someone.

2. CHECK OUT SOCIAL NETWORKING. Any candidate you are seriously considering for hire should also be checked on Facebook, MySpace, LinkedIn, Twitter, and other social media platforms for any potentially derogatory or inflammatory information.

3. TAKE YOUR TIME TO FIND THE RIGHT FIT. Take your time in screening and interviewing candidates when looking for talent to work in your agency. Hiring represents a significant commitment on your part as an employer and it's nothing you should hurry along. Be patient and hire slowly. Recognize that your first hire into a position may not be the last hire you make for that position. Oftentimes, it takes several hires before the right fit for the position is discovered. Don't despair at the time it takes to find the right person for the position. Trying to rehabilitate or change an under-performing employee is oftentimes a futile effort. It is often best to terminate their employment and begin the process of finding the right candidate for the position. Never be in a hurry to commit relatively large sums of money and additional emotional and intellectual equity into someone. The process of

hiring must be a deliberate process, not a random one. It must also be a cautious process, without urgency if at all possible.

4. FAIL YOUR FAILURES FAST. People reveal themselves rather quickly as a general rule. If the omens or vibes are not good—that is, if the new hire's performance is subpar early on in the onboarding process as a new employee—it is usually indicative of future long-term behavior/work performance problems. In such cases, I would consider decisively making the decision to fire them early in their tenure. Always incorporate a probationary period of thirty, sixty, or ninety days with a new hire.

5. SCREEN RESUMES CAREFULLY. Resumes should have no other purpose for the hiring agent than as a tool to determine if a prospective candidate warrants a closer 'look' by way of a formal interview or not. To subscribe any other purpose for a resume is to invite unnecessary problems into the recruiting and selection process. When screening resumes, consider the following:

a.) Misspellings on a resume are unacceptable in this era of spell-check programs, which are available to anyone
b.) Bizarre email addresses on a resume are unacceptable. Email addresses are free through the Internet. If a candidate doesn't have a professional- or mature- sounding email address, don't consider them a viable candidate.
c.) Question significant gaps in employment and/or short employment tenures that allude to job hopping.
d.) When calling on resumes, bizarre voicemail greetings should eliminate individuals as candidates for consideration.

6. DON'T GET MARRIED. Recruiting and hiring is a lot like buying and selling a stock on the New York Stock Exchange. Too often, once an investor decides on a stock and purchases it, they become 'married' to it, in a sense. A common investor error is to hold on to a stock even when it is performing poorly. Even when every indicator is suggesting that the investor minimize their losses by selling at a price lower than they had originally purchased the stock, the investor can't let go because of emotional attachment. Ignoring the market indicators and the expert advice while at the

Pull Your Nose Up

same time hoping against hope that the stock's performance will improve is a mistake. In the end, the losses the investor might have sustained yesterday pale in comparison to the losses they face from waiting too long to sell today.

In similar fashion, a new hire that under-performs is like a stock that is under-performing. It is okay to fire someone who is not performing in the position they were hired to fulfill. In some respects, it is inconsiderate of the agent-owner to create hope against hope in the heart of the under-performing employee by keeping them onboard. Most individuals who are under-performing know it already, and firing them can be the kindest thing you can do for them.

7. ENCOURAGE YOUR EMPLOYEES TO INVEST . Without investment, there is no commitment to success. Get your employee invested in the agency, and you will create an employee who is committed to success and excellence in the agency. Investment is accomplished in one of three ways: by way of money, time, and ideas. Most employees are reluctant to invest their own money in the success of the agency, but many will invest additional time and effort, as well as their ideas on how to improve agency operations. Solicit from your employees their ideas. They will be eager to share them with you if they are sincerely requested. In regard to time and effort, assign them projects and responsibilities that will provide them with a reasonable chance of success followed by recognition and reward. Investment is the only way to garner an individual's commitment to success—the ONLY way.

8. HOLD REGULAR MEETINGS. Hold regular office-business meetings with your employees to accomplish four major things: shape employee thinking, gain understanding and agreement on issues, secure investment and commitment, and training on new products and procedures. Consider involving each employee in the presenting (investing) of topics that fall under each category. Rotate these responsibilities and be eager to recognize everyone for their positive contributions to the agency's success. Office-business meetings are excellent forums to secure employee commitment for success.

9. DEPERSONALIZE. Depersonalize the performance management of your employees by using job descriptions, staff handbooks, and agreed-upon goals and production reports whenever having performance discussions with them.

10. WHAT GETS MEASURED GETS DONE. Measure what it is you want your employees to accomplish for you. Utilize available production reports and review them regularly with your staff. A good forum to have such discussions is during office-business meetings.

11. REWARD THE BEHAVIOR YOU WANT REPEATED. Reward desired employee behavior, and it will get repeated over and over again.

12. EXPECT EXCELLENCE, BUT BE REASONABLE. People rise to the expectation you have in them, so expect excellence and let them know you believe in their abilities to achieve excellence. Be sure to remain reasonable in your expectations. Don't burden them with things you would not be willing to take upon yourself if needed.

16. ALWAYS HONOR YOUR COMMITMENTS TO COMPENSATION AND BENEFITS. There are two things an employer should maintain heightened awareness and sensitivity towards or else risk losing employee loyalty and commitment to success; the two things are their earned time-off and their earned pay. Be as accommodating as possible with an employee's vacation/time-off and never, ever delay or refuse to pay what they are owed. If there is a disagreement or misunderstanding regarding pay between an employee and you, resolve it immediately and amicably. To do otherwise will invite untold employee-employer problems.

17. REWARD GOOD JUDGMENT AND SHARE THE DECISION-MAKING AUTHORITY. Drive decision-making authority to the lowest level in your agency as is possible in order to better serve your customers and to be more efficient as

Pull Your Nose Up

a business operation. Do this with caution, however, and never give an employee the responsibility to make decisions on behalf of customers or the agency until they have proven themselves worthy of good judgment in using such authority. "Prove them in order to approve them" is an excellent axiom to follow when it comes to deciding who should…decide.

The hiring and management of agency employees is one of the most difficult tasks the agent-owner faces. Follow the advice laid out in these pages and avoid unnecessary expense, time, effort, and heartache when it comes to hiring and managing your employees effectively.

Create a Detailed Staff Team Handbook & Job Description

Why bother to create a staff handbook or write a detailed job description for each position within the agency? Because these are the tools an agent uses to acquire new talent into the organization and manage that talent once they are integrated into the operations of the business.

A detailed handbook outlines everything: vacation and sick-time rules, production expectations, tasks, office policies, rewards and recognition, pay and benefits, and other items. A detailed job description, on the other hand, defines the tasks and expectations for a given position that must be performed in order for the agency to function and prosper.

Detailed job descriptions also help to avoid any misunderstandings between the employer (agent) and the employee (staff) when it comes to those issues important to both parties.

"To be understood is a luxury." ~ Henry Wadsworth Longfellow

A detailed handbook and job description becomes the standard by which you select the right person for the right position, and these are the platform from which you manage and shape employee behaviors and outcomes, all within a framework of mutual understanding and agreement. They are effective tools to use or refer to during:

1. One-on-one performance evaluation discussions
2. Team meetings when discussing staff-team policy and procedures
3. When on-boarding a new hire and establishing expectations
4. Recruiting, interviewing, and training efforts
5. Team conflict, misunderstandings, or disagreements

Though these tools are often overlooked by small business owners, utilizing such tools will serve you well.

These inject objectivity into the recruiting process, ensuring further that a hiring decision is made in alignment with what the business unit needs and not necessarily what the business unit wants.

Additionally, these tools also depersonalize any coaching or counseling moments based on performance because objectivity, once again, is maintained. Any coaching conversation will stay within the bounds of objective performance outcomes and not irrelevant, subjective opinion.

Hire Attitude-Aptitude-Appearance

Attitude: I can't put the 'fire in the belly', or the burning motivational drive to succeed, into an individual. It needs to be there already. Motivation and attitude go hand in hand and are inseparable by nature. Each can be influenced and the spark fanned into a flame that will drive an individual to achieve and go beyond the norm of what most people believe is possible.

But if there is no hint of a spark of motivation or a positive and open attitude toward learning and change, any effort to coach someone to excellence will be met only with disappointment and regret in hiring them at all. A good attitude is something someone either has or does not. Don't waste your time with the latter. Hire attitude! If you hire anything less, you will be hiring a problem, plain and simple.

Aptitude: Selling insurance and financial products takes some intellectual horsepower; in other words, it takes someone with a good mind and the ability to learn quickly and perform effectively in order to be successful. Hire smart and let the other guy hire… stupid.

Appearance: I am not suggesting you hire a super-model or individual who has walked off the cover of a fashion magazine (although that wouldn't hurt). I am suggesting you hire someone who is professional-looking, someone who projects the public image you would like your agency or small business to be known and branded for in the community.

Anthony D. Cefalu

Every employee of an organization represents that organization, whether they realize this fact or not. Perception is reality, and customer perception is what matters most to the success of your business.

Attitude, aptitude, and appearance, the three things to look for when recruiting talent.

Expectations and Outcomes

Every company has its methods of measuring results or outcomes in classic reports fashion. Oftentimes, the multitude of measurements and reports a company provides for its people is overwhelming.

At the small business owner level, getting trapped in a sea of endless reports on things such as production, expenses, schedules, payroll, bonuses, charge backs, taxes, supplies and billing, just to name a few, is frustrating and a huge drag on business activity.

The value of certain metrics, or reports, is directly proportionate to the purpose they serve in helping you meet your business goals.

What does this have to do with staffing issues? A lot, particularly as they relate to employee performance and overall business success.

Managing the performance of employees within any organization is a challenge. Here are some important tips that can help you manage them more effectively:

1. DEFINE THE ROLE. Define in detail the role of the position needing filled. Be clear about expectations, tasks, skill levels, and production or service goals. In fact, make this a part of your employee handbook or manual, in which all manner of issues regarding pay and personal time off are addressed and detailed. Thoroughly reviewing an employee handbook and job description

with staff minimizes the risk of any misunderstanding arising between employer and employee. Again, hire to the position and not the person; all too often business owners fail to hire this way. Don't make the same mistake.

2. ESTABLISH GOALS. Once you have defined and described the position in detail, the next thing is to establish specific goals for the position (e.g. number of sales expected per month). Detailing the processes and tasks defines what behaviors are expected for the position; setting goals defines the expected outcomes as a result of those behaviors.

3. COMPARE OUTCOMES AND EXPECTATIONS. The final piece of the performance management challenge is to compare actual outcomes to expected outcomes. This is accomplished by taking the metrics and reports available to you that identify the employees actual outcomes to the goals you established for them earlier in the job description and/or the employee handbook. Having employee goals allows for the effective management of an employee. To ignore the necessity for clearly established, written goals allows for the possibility of employee performance problems to develop.

A detailed job description, an employee handbook, and goals are absolutely crucial to effective performance management. Such tools serve to depersonalize the coaching discussions and help to keep the performance evaluation moments on an objective plain as much as possible.

They also prevent the coaching discussion from becoming one that breaches the boundaries of appropriateness and legality between owner and employee.

> Job Description + Employee Handbook + Written Performance Goals = Anticipated Outcomes
>
> The use of metrics, or reports, illustrating the individual's actual work results = Actual Outcomes

It is in the space between expected outcomes and actual outcomes that the employee performance discussion must be constructed in order to be effective.

When performance management discussions focus on work-related behaviors and competencies rather than subjective personal opinion issues, the coaching and evaluation moment is better received and has a greater likelihood of affecting the behavior of the employee in a positive direction for the business unit.

In summary, effective and profitable employee performance management is governed, framed, and implemented by using the following tools:

EXPECTATIONS are established

1. Employee Handbook/Manual
2. Detailed Job Description
3. Written Goals for the Employee

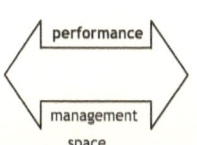

OUTCOMES are measured

1. Available Metrics/Reports to determine the actual employee outcome or Production

To grow your business and influence your employees so they will execute on processes the business unit needs and the position requires, manage to employee behaviors in the space between expectations and actual outcomes. Any other method of managing your employees is ineffective in creating a sales culture in your agency or small business.

Don't Fall in Love and Other Words-of-Wisdom

1. If a resume says loverboy@xxxx.com or something similarly inappropriate, the candidate is probably immature. All the major Internet search engines offer free email service and addresses. If the candidate has no situational awareness about securing a respectable and mature email address, they are just too unaware to be considered for hire.

2. If the candidate's resume indicates significant gaps in work history, you should most definitely inquire about these gaps. Likewise, if they have a work history that indicates a lack of continuity or longevity with employers, find out why they have had so many different employers.

3. If a candidate's voicemail greeting is strange and inappropriate, you should reconsider whether you want to interview them or not.

4. If a candidate presents an image in Facebook, MySpace, Twitter, Plaxo, or any other social media outlet that would not reflect well on your business in terms of marketplace perception, don't consider them for hire.

5. If there are misspellings on the resume, don't consider them for hire—especially in an era of spell-check availability.

6. If a candidate shows up to the interview looking unprofessional, do not consider them for hire, end of story. They get no do-overs. In such cases, it is a five-minute courtesy interview, a "Thank you for coming in" before I walk them to the exit, never doubting that I made the right decision. A candidate without enough self-respect and dignity to dress and groom properly for a professional environment or one who lacks the situational awareness and common sense to look appropriate for an interview has absolutely no place in a business environment of mine, and they shouldn't have a place in your business either. I do understand that some candidates may not have the financial means to buy an expensive interview outfit. As business owners, we need to be sensitive to such situations and base our decisions on the person and not on appearance only, but I do insist that appearance is part of who someone is, and perception speaks to customer reactions, good or bad. Individuals can still look neat, clean, groomed, and professional for an interview without having to spend money they do not have on an interview outfit.

7. The interview is what I consider 'game day'. If the candidate does not present well in the interview, too bad for them. It may sound harsh, but that is how I look at it. It is their one chance to shine, so to speak, to impress me with their qualifications. I don't seek perfection from the candidate during an interview, but I do expect the following minimum standards to be observed by any candidate worth considering for hire:

   a. To be on time for the interview
   b. To display maturity in demeanor and conversation
   c. To have prepared for the interview
   d. To demonstrate a positive attitude about the position and with working with people
   e. To possess the requisite aptitude to learn the job and develop the necessary skills required for the position
   f. To have a professional appearance

If a candidate falls short in these areas, do not make excuses for them. If you do, it will result in a bad hiring choice in the end.

8. If a candidate asks for the job at the interview conclusion, I interpret that as a favorable indicator of success and job suitability, especially when looking to fill a sales position within my agency.

9. Design a structured approach to the interview. Be deliberate in your questioning. Ask open-ended behavioral or competency-based questions to elicit the following three elements in a candidate's answer:

   a. An explanation of the circumstances or example in question—the problem or obstacles the candidate was challenged with overcoming
   b. The reaction or action taken by the individual as a result of the circumstance
   c. The outcomes of the candidate's actions.

An example interview question might look like the following

"Describe for me a time when you were given a challenging sales goal to achieve. What were the circumstances, and what steps did you take in response to the challenge? What was the outcome of your actions?"

10. An interview needs to be as *long* as necessary to thoroughly gauge the fitness of an individual for a given position. I would also urge you to be mindful of what I refer to as a 'new law of gravity' when it comes to interviewing candidates.

In the past, I have observed long, grueling interviews led by business owners (insurance agent-owners) for positions that would be considered entry-level jobs, relatively low-paying positions requiring no experience and no skills. Even though they were for entry-level positions, some of these interviews lasted as long as two hours. Because of the inordinate length of the interview, I wondered if I was assessing a candidate for a CEO position of a Fortune 500 company rather than a part-time telemarketing position!

Be reasonable as a business owner and interviewer. For the gravity or relative impact and weight a telemarketing position has on a small business operation, a two-hour interview is unwarranted and inappropriate. In fact, in some past instances, I have been surprised that the candidate didn't walk out on the interviewer because of the issue of gravity.

Interviews are not meant to be engagements in attrition between the interviewer and candidate to see who wears out first or who runs out of questions and answers first. They are structured forums designed to assess an individual's fitness to perform the duties of a particular position... and nothing more. They are most certainly not forums to satisfy an interviewer's inappropriate curiosity about someone else or to satisfy any personal ego drive or need. Interviews should be focused on business and performance issues at work, but they should be as long as necessary and as short as possible in order to find out what you need to know about the candidate.

11. Sometimes, what can occur during an interview is a phenomenon I call 'falling in love'. This is an occurrence the interviewer falls prey to during the actual interview itself when a candidate—for whatever reason—suddenly becomes the darling of the interviewer. What little logic that was being used to assess the candidate's fitness for the position is extinguished and suddenly exchanged for emotions and gut feelings in making the final hiring decision. Its victims are often oblivious to the affects that falling in love has on them during an interview, but others see it. It usually starts with an excessive amount of attention paid by the interviewer on the candidate.

Overt symptoms of this phenomenon can be seen when the interview conversation drifts from the formal questioning of a structured process to the realm of familiar comments and opinions, usually solicited by the interviewer of the candidate. Invariably, the interviewer's questions can morph into a series of compliments and helpful comments to dismiss away any deficiencies once noted in the candidate's qualifications for the job.

Don't fall in love with a candidate for hire—at least not during

Pull Your Nose Up

the interview. No matter how impressive the individual is, it is not wise to allow your body language or your words to communicate that they are a favored candidate for the position. Adopting a formal, structured interview process with predetermined and deliberate questions to the candidate will help you to avoid this common pitfall of business owners.

Staff issues are always a challenge for the agent-owner. The above tips are meant to be helpful and not harmful to anyone, including those individuals being considered for employment.

To Diet or Not to Diet?

One of the biggest challenges facing the agency-owner is expense management—making sure expenses don't exceed revenues or outpace a business owner's ability to pay those expenses on time.

Paying the bills when vendors and suppliers demand to be paid is a critical element of staying in business. If expenses and the demand to have them paid precedes the ability of the agent-owner to pay them on time, the business will die financially. It may die a slow death, so to speak, but it will eventually die nonetheless. Why? Because of inadequate cash flow.

CASH FLOW IS KING TO THE SMALL BUSINESS OWNER

This is why cash flow is king to the small business owner. Not only is the ability to pay the bills important, but the ability to pay them on time is just as critical to business survival.

YOU ARE WHAT YOU EAT WHEN IT COMES TO EXPENSES

Oftentimes, the source of our financial difficulties as business owners or agent-owners lies within our ability to control and resolve. Most of our challenges in business are not dominated by forces unseen or are not unpredictable in nature.

No, the things that challenge us most of the time are like a diet.

If a person consistently ignores the effects excessive amounts of food intake and fat have on their health and overall lifespan, they will eventually suffer the consequences of their actions by way of a physical collapse or major medical event that isn't going to be good for them. It isn't the Twinkie® that kills a person; it's the eating of excessive amounts of Twinkies®.

ARE YOU A TWINKIE® EATER?

As the expression goes, "You are what you eat." In application to the business arena, we become what we consume our time, money, and energies on. Our actions are predictive of our future outcomes. Eat too many sugar-laced foods, and the outcome will be a body indicative of excessive sugar intake… and we all know what that looks like.

Similarly, if you spend (consume) excessive amounts of precious capital resources on items that have little or nothing to do with marketing and selling insurance, the outcome will be reflective of an agency void of a sales and marketing culture.

The converse is also true. If you spend your money in areas that will drive customers to your storefront and help retain them, the outcome will be a business unit that is growing and is adaptable to the marketplace—an agency capable of untold revenue generation. That kind of expense management creates a sales culture within your agency that will be the envy of your competition.

TO DIET OR NOT TO DIET? THAT IS THE QUESTION

It is an irrefutable law of life that for every action, there is an attendant result or equal and opposite reaction as an outcome. Agent-owners who drain precious capital resources on things that have no firm business purpose risk becoming increasingly weakened financially, exposing themselves to growing cash flow problems.

Pull Your Nose Up

What this all means for any business owner who is struggling to be profitable and grow is this: "Do I go on a diet or not, financially speaking?"

If you are worried about expenses and honestly have no methodology or plan in place to manage those expenses, my recommendations is a simple one: GO ON A DIET!

Diets are not fun. All too often, they are either too complicated to be practical or they make unrealistic claims of nearly effortless and dramatic weight loss. It is rarely for lack of desire that someone doesn't lose weight. The reason many people abandon diets and realize little weight loss is for lack of having a simple plan to follow and the discipline to execute regularly on that plan.

"Entities must not be multiplied beyond necessity" ~ William of Ockham, Fourteenth-century English Logician, Theologian, and Franciscan Friar

It is unreasonable to adopt a diet strategy that is so restrictive it robs a person of their energy and the ability to sustain a certain weight once that goal has been reached. It is equally unreasonable to think someone can lose weight without ever being deliberate and disciplined about it. So what is the solution?

In the fourteenth century, a principle of logic applicable to the sciences, the arts, business, and all endeavors, for that matter was devised. This principle was called 'Occam's Razor', and it stated, "The simplest solution to a problem is usually the correct one." Entities must not be multiplied beyond necessity. In simple English, that translates into, "Keep it simple, stupid."

Too often, problems that appear to be complex are really simple to understand and have attendant solutions that are just as simple.

Anthony D. Cefalu

EXPENSE MANAGEMENT IS ABOUT SIMPLICITY & DISCIPLINE AND NOTHING MORE

Effective expense management is comprised of two elements: a simple plan and the discipline to work that plan, just like in dieting.

Two questions comprise the expense management plan:

1. Does what I am considering to spend money on **directly drive prospects (marketing)** to the place where I transact business or support sales in anyway (e.g. store front, phone number, web portal)?

    If the answer is "yes," spend the money and make sure you monitor the *return on investment* of that particular expenditure. If the return on investment is not enough to justify the expense—or worse yet, a negative effect on the business—discontinue spending money on that process or system right away.

    If the answer is "no," you have to ask yourself a second question, which is:

2. If the expense I am considering to incur does not directly drive marketing activities or the sales process, is it an expense that will **support** these two functions of an agency in some way?

    If the answer again is "no," don't spend the money. It's that simple. An insurance agency is a business organization, yes, but it also operates as an organism with living, breathing individuals driving the processes within it and steering its activity in a deliberate fashion.

    Therefore, it is important to recognize the need to keep that organism healthy by maintaining a focus on driving marketing and sales activities first and all other activities second.

BUT THAT COSTS MONEY!

An organization requires support in many different forms: fax machines, computers telephone systems, lights, chairs, desks, and other items. The challenge with such spending is to resist the urge to spend excessive amounts of capital resources on them and other less essential things.

SIMPLICITY & DISCIPLINE

Solid business principles matter. They are the foundations from which all good business processes spring forth and flourish. Without principles, an endeavor, an idea, a process, or a person is a flawed product—something less than what it or they could have been.

When considering expense management as a business owner and the critical function of making sure money is spent on the business where money is needed, the responsibility can be daunting and confusing. If not daunting or confusing, managing expenses and paying the bills is at least frustrating.

But, it really is not all that difficult of a task—at least the process isn't. Just ask yourself two simple questions. That's all! That is the entire process, and nothing more, and it can't get any simpler.

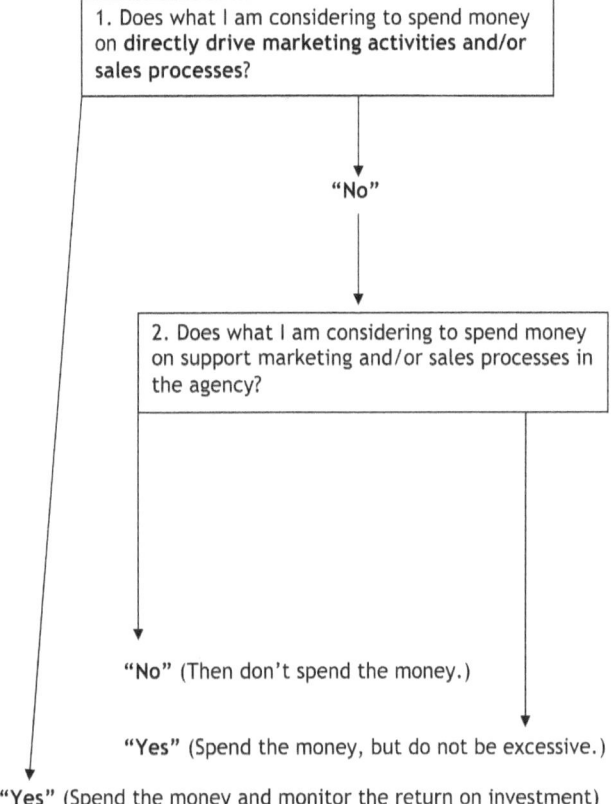

The hard part to this entire discussion is the need for discipline, specifically the discipline to ask yourself the two questions and the discipline to adhere to the ultimate answer for each.

Do you want to get control of business spending issues? Is cash flow a problem for you as a business owner? Can you use some help in getting rid of wasteful spending in order to improve your cash flow situation? Would you like to free up money that is available to you? Then take my advice: Go on a diet!

Control Your Calendar Before It Controls You

"The goal is to balance a life that works with a life that counts." ~ Peter Block, The Answer to How is Yes

It has been said time is the most precious commodity we possess. Everyone has it gifted to them, and everyone has it at their disposal to choose what to do and when they want to do it.

Certainly, there are circumstances in life where our time is not our own. But on balance, it is the one thing we all possess—rich and poor, male and female. All of us have time. What you do with the time you have is a different story.

"Time is the coin of your life. It is the only coin you have, and only you can determine how it will be spent. Be careful lest you let other people spend it for you." ~ Carl Sandburg, Writer, Poet, Philosopher

One of the most challenging aspects of the sales profession is managing the time we are given in order to sell, market, run a business, and maintain a balanced personal life. If the sales professional's day consistently means working from nine a.m. to nine p.m. Monday through Friday (or even Monday through Saturday in many instances) a mental and/or emotional breakdown will occur. That is why it is so important to control your calendar.

"Doing too much has always been a serious problem. It's no coincidence that most heart attacks occur at nine a.m. on Monday morning. (So much for the masochistic maxim, 'Hard work never killed anyone'.)" ~ Bradley Trevor Grieve, *The Book for People Who do Too Much*

It's an easy thing to let one's profession consume them with tasks, appointments, meetings, payroll, marketing, complaints, taxes, insurance, quotas, bookkeeping, maintenance, purchasing, travel, reports, training, and customer service issues, to name a few. And in the sales profession, there seems to be a particular tendency to let the details of the job overwhelm us and cause us to do too much too often, oftentimes at the cost of maintaining a balanced personal and family life.

The folly of a "hard work never killed anyone" attitude is that it ignores the importance of working and living a balanced life in order to maximize one's production. It puts the sales professional at risk of being a slave to the job, to the whims and schedules of customers and other people, and it breeds within the heart and mind of the sales expert an unhealthy frustration and contempt with never being able to do personal things.

It is a recipe for disaster professionally and personally for anyone who allows their work to consume their private time, their me-time.

The following are some suggestions for controlling your calendar in order to ensure you are happy at work and at home:

1. Specifically plan out your work hours and activities. This includes the use of your cell phone, Blackberry, and email. The paradox within the technology realm is that technology has helped business people become more efficient through accessibility, but it has also helped us to be less effective through accessibility as well.

Pull Your Nose Up

You must specifically define protocols for *when* and under *what* circumstances you will use these electronic tools in order to get your work done. Otherwise, they will soon become tools that create for you an additional burden through constant, unrestrained availability.

When relaxing and recharging physically and mentally, turn these things off. Breach this rule only in the case of an emergency. You'll relax better, feel better, and avoid being a slave to everyone else's calendar and whims if you leverage technology for a specific business purpose during specific work times.

2. Decide how you will plot out your work week appointments, meetings, and other activities. Get control of your appointment calendar. Do not let others, even customers, tell you when you are going to work. I agree that sales professionals need to be flexible with their appointment book, but only to a reasonable point.

   It is quite normal for any business professional to maintain a personal life outside of the office. Don't allow others to be unreasonable with your personal time.

   Decide what nights and weekends you will meet by appointment. Adjust your appointment calendar on the fly. That is, if you have a five-p.m. appointment on a given day and another appointment two hours later at seven p.m. that same evening, work to compress that calendar. Why wait an hour or longer to see your seven-p.m. prospect once you have concluded your earlier appointment?

   Instead, call the seven o'clock appointment and say, "I have an opening that came available at six, so if you would like to come in earlier you can. How does that sound?" Controlling your calendar allows you to be home that much sooner, no longer a slave to someone else's calendar, but a master of your own calendar and time.

In the previous scenario, the customer may agree to moving their appointment up to an earlier time. If so, it is better for you, but you will never know if they will make the change in appointment time unless you ask them. Don't be afraid to ask. Being flexible with customers and with your appointment calendar is a necessity, but don't sacrifice control over your time and your life at the altar of always accommodating the calendars and times of other people. There needs to be some balance and reason applied to the decision of when you will… and when you will not work.

3. When you are at work, be at work. When away from work, be away from work. You'll thank me for this advice if you follow it.

HAPPINESS IS A CHOICE THAT REQUIRES EFFORT

This thinking promotes a focus of energy, economy of effort, and efficiency of activities. Freedom—particularly for the insurance and financial services professional—can be deadly to a career that does not operate within the context of discipline.

Be disciplined and focus on your marketing and sales activities in order to be successful and happy. Write out your schedule and tasks and be deliberate in executing on what must get done as a result.

A person who doesn't *plan their work and work their plan* is asking for problems and frustration, and it will cause you to waste a lot of time when you could be getting things done during the work day. If it doesn't get done during working hours, it will intrude upon your personal time. Is that how you want to work and live all of your life?

ONE THING YOU CANNOT RECYCLE IS WASTED TIME

4. Specifically program into your work day some time for self-

Pull Your Nose Up

development. Understand your professional needs for your own growth and development as a sales expert and/or business owner. Programming one to two hours into every week so you can leave the sales environment and invest time in yourself to stay mentally and physically sharp is important for any professional.

Read a book, attend a seminar, or watch a film/DVD, for example, on a related professional topic. These kinds of activities help an individual to recharge their mental batteries and discover new ideas about sales, marketing, and operating a business.

You will feel better and gain a greater sense of purpose and accomplishment if you take time to invest in your own professional and personal growth.

Allowing the busy-ness of running a business to get in the way of your own development is a recipe for increased work stress and discontent. You will feel more relaxed if you feed your own mental and emotional needs by programming self-development time into your work week.

A FINAL NOTE

An agent friend of mine decided early in his career that he was going to have control over his calendar and not vice versa. He was a young man, a single father in his early thirties. He wanted to have a successful career and, at the same time, be the kind of father he wanted to be to his only child, a son. In other words, he wanted to be able to sell insurance and financial services products and sell them well as a top performer, while at the same time coaching his son's baseball team, a tall order for a new agent trying to build a business.

Faced with having to meet stringent sales targets while at the same time being a coach for his son, he determined to plan out his work week specifically and to program time into his week for self-development activities as well.

The work hours he set for himself were clearly defined. He worked nine to five on Monday, Thursday, and Friday. Tuesday and Wednesday, he came into the office and work from noon until eight p.m. As for Saturdays, he almost never worked them unless it was an absolute necessity or he felt the prospect was a serious shopper needing help and was simply unable to meet at any other time.

The result? He was the number one life sales professional nationally his first two years selling in an organization that has thousands of professional vying for such a distinction. Later, his sales responsibilities expanded, and he is now a top producer year in and year out for his company. The interesting thing about him was that he was always cheerful, always positive, and always had time to help people and to speak to large sales groups about his success.

In summary, this is what he told sales and business professionals:

1. I keep work time, work time and me time, me time… and the two rarely spill over into each other. I am clear on my work hours with customers and assume they will adjust their schedules to meet with me. Why? Because I am a professional and should be treated no less than any other busy professional.

   I am flexible and careful to be kind when I am unable to meet with someone on their first choice of times, but I am also determined about getting my work done during scheduled work hours. I am always able to reach a good compromise with people. It is a very rare instance when a prospect or client will not work with me to find a mutually agreeable time to meet.

2. When setting an appointment to meet with someone, I say; "My next available appointment is…" With this verbiage, there is an implied message that tells the individual, "I am a busy

Pull Your Nose Up

insurance and financial services professional." What I try to do is create scarcity, a powerful psychological tool that suggests that if you can't have something, or if it is in limited supply (i.e., appointment times to meet with me), a natural desire will arise within most individuals to want that scarce thing, which, in this case, is an appointment with me.

The Law of Mass Involvement, or herding instinct, is another psychological tool at play here as well. It states that if everyone is doing it (for example, coming to see me with an appointment), maybe they should as well.

Too many agents, particularly new agents, make the mistake of accommodating customers with an appointment time that is exceedingly convenient for the customer and equally inconvenient for the agent.

I have heard agents on the phone speaking to a prospect about setting an appointment to meet them, saying, "You tell me. I'll meet with you whenever you like. My schedule is wide open. Just name the date and time."

The agent that does that might as well be saying, "No one wants to meet with me. I'll do anything to get an appointment with you. Please! I am begging you, meet with me!"

If you sound desperate to meet a customer, you are desperate—or at least that is what the customer will perceive of you. On the other hand, when trying to schedule a meeting with a customer, if you sound busy and in demand, you are busy and in demand.

How do you want people to perceive you when persuading them to meet with you?

I understand why new agents fall prey to the temptation of being exceedingly accommodating with their time and calendar; it is because they need the sale or are up against a deadline when it comes to production requirements.

At times, being exceedingly accommodating with your calendar and time toward the customer is necessary in order to meet deadlines and production goals, but making accommodations to your calendar a regular habit is unhealthy personally and professionally for any career-minded person.

3. Cancelled appointments and 'no-shows' are looked upon as inventory for next week. Sure, no one likes cancelled appointments, but then, it is all in how you look at it. I see cancellations as opportunities to reset the appointment for the following week, thus helping me to get the requisite fifteen to twenty appointments for the upcoming week.

   It is all about perspective when looking at cancelled appointments. Many of my cancellations do reschedule, and many do eventually show up to the appointment and end up buying something.

4. I move appointments up when I can. If I have a six p.m. and an eight p.m. on the same night, I often call the same day and see if my customers would like to move their appointments up in order to make things more convenient for me.

5. I leverage the answer machine. If the prospect I am scheduled to meet is not home, the message goes something like, "Hi. This is Tim from Professional Insurance Consultants. I'm just calling about our eight-p.m. appointment tonight and to let you know I was able to meet with my seven p.m. earlier today, so that time slot is now available if you'd like to meet earlier, rather than at eight p.m. If you would like to meet at seven instead, just let me know by calling, xxx-xxx-xxxx. Otherwise, if I do not hear from you, I will be waiting here for you at eight as scheduled. Thank you."

   With such strategies as mentioned above, my friend was able to work his calendar and control his time, and he was a happier sales expert, business professional, and person as a result. Just remember, if you don't control your calendar, someone else will!

Game Maker...Or Game Breaker

"A bore is a person who talks when you wish him to listen." ~ *Ambrose Bierce*

Listening isn't just hearing. Listening isn't something passive, and it isn't waiting for your turn to talk either, which is what it seems to mean to many people.

In defining what exactly it means to be a listener, one has to consider the skill of listening as both an art form and as a discipline. Without a vivid imagination and the instincts to discern a person's feelings and emotional needs, it is very difficult for the sales professional to truly understand what a customer is saying and to find solutions that are the best fit for their needs.

Listening involves different variables. When people communicate, they not only use words to be understood, but they also use vocal devices such as volume, tone, and speed, along with body language. Therefore, being adept at listening to the customer and pinpointing their exact needs from the words they use, the sounds they make, and the gestures and body language they display is a skill that requires more than a simple insurance sales technician perspective on the sales profession.

It takes finesse and, at times, a reaction to gut feelings to master the skill of listening. It is an art, as I've said, to really hear what people are saying to you as a sales professional.

Anthony D. Cefalu

"To be understood is a luxury." ~ Henry Wadsworth Longfellow

As a discipline, listening to others is difficult work. We all have a natural tendency to be preoccupied with our own lives and our own individual thoughts and concerns. To silence that natural urge within us in order to be attentive to what other people are saying and wanting is nothing short of a deliberate act of discipline.

Listening is a learned behavior as well as an art form. It is something that has to be felt and sensed by the sales professional, as well as something that must be consciously practiced and exercised in order to be mastered.

In the sales arena, listening is a critical skill, if not THE critical skill, most sales professionals need to develop, exercise, practice, and master.

LISTEN PEOPLE INTO BUYING

Consider what the act of listening says about you as a professional and as an individual, from the perspective of the customer.

First, it tells the customer you care about them and about what they are thinking.

Whenever a person is allowed to speak, uninterrupted, it not only gives them a sense of liberation, but it also tells them you care about what they think, what they want, and what they need. In a sense, listening can be likened to a gift to the customer. Its effect is extremely powerful in bringing the discussion to a close or sale.

How does it make you feel when others give you their attention and time by listening intently to what you have to say about a matter? The answer is obvious: It makes you feel good.

Asked another way, How does it make you feel when others fail to be attentive to what you are saying or fail to give you their time by

Pull Your Nose Up

interrupting you when you are speaking on a matter? The answer to that question is just as obvious: It makes you feel bad.

So, how important is it to your success as a sales professional to give of your attention and your time, as I've mentioned, to customers and potential customers you come in contact with every day? Extremely important!

If customers do not feel good about you or your business, they will go somewhere else where they will be made to feel good, special, and cared for. That 'somewhere else' is your competition, and it's the last place you want your customers to go.

DIFFERENTIATE YOURSELF BY GIVING YOUR CUSTOMERS WHAT THEY WANT

What do customers want? They want to feel good about who they are and what they have purchased. Listening to someone accomplishes that task almost singlehandedly.

Just think of how powerfully persuasive you can be as an effective listener. The ability to make someone feel good and worthwhile has an almost addictive effect on a person.

What do your customers feel when they are with you in a conversation? Are you giving them what they want, or is the conversation more about what you want to accomplish and what you want to say when you are with a customer? The answer to these questions can define your level of success in the sales profession.

IGNORING SOMEONE IS THE UNFORGIVABLE SIN

When a person is made to feel ignored or is interrupted when they are speaking, they feel robbed of something. The sense of insult and disrespect a person experiences in such instances is often felt deeply and personally.

Anthony D. Cefalu

To interrupt or ignore what someone is saying—even by way of innocent daydreaming—is a naturally demeaning act that says to the one speaking, "You are not worthy to be heard or accounted for as someone who matters. What you think and say isn't important."

That's robbery of the most severe kind, a kind of sociologic robbery of an individual's dignity and self-worth. The only outcome for such a violation of a person's right to be heard comes from a litany of negative feelings experienced by the speaker: resentment, anger, hurt, frustration, impatience, and even vengefulness.

For some, what I have written sounds extreme and exaggerated. I can appreciate the fact that some individuals are not as sensitive or insulted when they are ignored or interrupted when they speak. To those individuals, I applaud you for your patience and tolerance of others and their shortcomings (no matter how unintended) in not being deliberate in listening to what you have to say at times. It is commendable and exceptional in respect to your patience and ability to forgive such rudeness.

But for the majority of people who are ignored, interrupted, or somehow dismissed for what they are saying, no matter what the excuse is for the insult, the resultant feeling the speaker experiences is not a good one.

Invalidate someone's worth as an individual by failing to listen effectively to them, and they will rarely ever forgive you for such a deep and personal violation of their dignity. It is a game breaker for the sales professional to fail to listen to customers and prospects.

HAVE YOU GOT GAME…WHEN IT COMES TO LISTENING?

"It struck me so forcibly that I shall never forget him. He had qualities which I had never seen in any other man. Never had I seen such concentrated attention. There was none of that piercing soul penetrating gaze business. His eyes were mild and genial. His voice was low and kind. His gestures were few. But the attention he gave

Pull Your Nose Up

me, his appreciation of what I said, even when I said it badly, was extraordinary. You've no idea what it meant to be listened to like that." ~ Dale Carnegie, *How to Win Friends and Influence People*, in regard to a patient's impression of Sigmund Freud

In order to be a good listener, it is important to give highlighted attention to the person speaking. Avoid preoccupation when interacting with customers. Think of the speaker, what they are saying, the tone of their voice, and their body language. Immerse yourself in their world and be interested in them and what is being said.

"Listening isn't just hearing. It's also understanding. It's understanding feelings and emotions. It's picking up subtle voice inflections and meanings. It's observing what people do with their hands and eyes—the congruence of their body language with their words." ~ Ron Willingham, *Hey, I'm the Customer*

Avoiding preoccupation when listening to a customer can be very difficult. It takes practice and discipline, but it is a necessary skill that the sales professional must develop in order to be successful.

How, then, do we avoid such dangers and improve upon our listening skills? The answer is simple:

1. Look people in the eye when speaking to them and listening. This will help you to stay attentive to what is being said, and it will keep you and the speaker engaged in conversation.

   "People who are really listening to you look into your eyes. Said another way, when people aren't looking into your eyes, it's virtually impossible for them to hear everything you're trying to tell them. Said yet another way, when people are preoccupied, they almost never keep total eye contact... when you force direct eye contact you'll not be preoccupied." ~ Ron Willingham, *Hey, I'm the Customer*

   Look people in the eye. That simple act is one of the most

powerful techniques a sales professional can employ in order to improve their listening skills. I challenge you to observe other sales professionals you come across in your daily activities of mall shopping, car buying, or whatever it may be. See if other sales professionals look you in the eye when speaking to you. Try to remember how they make you feel in those instances when they do look at you with highlighted attention… and when they don't.

2. Don't allow your conversations to be interrupted or distracted. As much as is possible, avoid interrupting telephone calls, text messages, email, or intrusions into your conversation by other people. Focus on the person speaking. Make them the most important person to you in that moment. They will love you for it.

3. Get used to acknowledging what is being said, asking clarifying questions, and making restatements of what you think they have just said from time to time. This will help you maintain your attention and improve your understanding about what is being said.

4. When appropriate, takes notes during a conversation. This tells the speaker that you are engaged and interested in what they are saying. It also helps you to recall the details of a conversation later.

"When you get good at listening to people, you'll tower above others who try to get your customer's money." ~ Ron Willingham, *Hey, I'm the Customer*

Tower over your competition by giving customers what they want: a listening ear.

Gone Without a Complaint

I hate having to handle complaints. Often, they are unpleasant experiences for both the sales professional and the *complaining customer*. Thus, the natural inclination of most individuals is to avoid dealing with them or to pass them on to someone else to resolve. But my counsel to anyone in sales—and anyone in business—is to embrace complaints and even invite them.

WELCOME THE COMPLAINER

Consider what a complaint really is from the customer's viewpoint: a plea by the customer to continue to do business with you.

Customers want to be heard and desire to be validated for how they feel. Complaining is the means by which they sometimes accomplish that end. In other words, when a customer complains, they are experiencing a diminished sense of value as a result of a perceived problem. The complaint is a way for them to regain that value, to let you know this, and to have you earn back their trust.

RE-EARN, RE-ESTABLISH, AND REINFORCE

Complaints are a wonderful opportunity for a sales professional to re-earn, re-establish, and reinforce why the customer ever bought from you in the first place. When viewed in the right perspective, a complaint is another opportunity to showcase your value as an agent, business owner, and trusted advisor to your customers. Your actions to resolve a complaint will only result in increased customer loyalty and satisfaction.

I never worry about the complaining customer. It is the customer who doesn't complain that worries me.

GONE WITHOUT A COMPLAINT

I fear having customers who leave quietly, almost secretly, and without ever giving anyone the chance to make things right.

A COMPLAINT STRATEGY TO CONSIDER: ACKNOWLEDGE, APPRECIATE, APOLOGIZE, ASSURE, & ANALYZE

<u>Acknowledge</u> the complaint regardless of its weight or validity. Don't consider whether the complaint is important or legitimate; just consider its value in being able to create immediate connection and rapport with the customer. Make them feel valued and comfortable with expressing themselves to you by listening intently to what they have to say.

Some ways to acknowledge a complaint might include:
"I can appreciate how you might feel…"
"I can understand why you would say that…"
"I see what you are saying…"

Notice that I do not suggest you agree with the complaint. Just acknowledge it for what it is and for the person making it.

<u>Appreciate</u> their feedback. "Thank you" by itself is a hollow gesture. Qualify it by stating what it is you are thankful about.

For example:
"Thank you for letting me know about this problem. It will help me to better serve you in the future."

Pull Your Nose Up

<u>Apologize</u> for the problem. "I'm sorry this happened," or "I apologize for the inconvenience," are simple and sincere expressions of regret. "I'm sorry" is a magic phrase that can only steer a negative conversation closer to a positive resolution. Overlook this component in handling a complaint, and you have missed one of the most powerful opportunities to gain a customer's loyalty.

<u>Assure</u> the customer you will address the complaint immediately. Assuring the customer you will help them with their problem will bring any natural tension in the conversation to a more relaxed level.

For example:
"I can assure you I'll do my best to correct this problem for you…"
"I will endeavor to take care of this situation as soon as possible…"
"I promise I will let the agent know right away so this can be resolved for you."

Always try to resolve the problem as quickly as possible. In those instances where you can't fix a problem immediately, let the customer know and explain what you will be able to do for them in the meantime. Follow up with the customer as appropriate.

<u>Analyze</u> the basis for the complaint. Fix the problem, fix the process, and/or fix the systems that are the source of the customer's complaint. Keep in mind that complaints can be a positive element to improving your marketing systems and business operations. Analyze the complaint on the basis of specific activities, processes, and systems. The worst way to analyze a problem is to personalize the source of the complaint or blame someone else for the problem. Keep your analysis focused on behaviors and actions versus people. This approach will help you to avoid repeat complaints about the same issue.

Anthony D. Cefalu

HANDLING A COMPLAINT IN SUMMARY

Acknowledge:	"I can appreciate how you feel, Mr. Smith."
Appreciate:	"Thank you for calling. Your feedback will help me to better serve you in the future."
Apologize:	"I do apologize for the inconvenience this has caused you…"
Assure:	"…and I can assure you, I will follow up as soon as I can with the claims department for you. Since it so late in the day, I may not be able to get in touch with a manager right away, but I will try. If I'm not able, I will call first thing tomorrow morning. Will that be alright with you?"

Complaints can be either a blessing or a curse, depending upon how they are handled. Formalize your complaint-handling strategy, and you will turn a seemingly negative situation into a marketing gem.

Don't Boil the Ocean

One of the great frustrations agents experience, particularly new agents, is the overwhelming sense to do everything necessary to be successful all at once. Because of our action-oriented natures as sales professionals, it's a common affliction among our ranks that can plague the mental health of an otherwise talented and promising agent.

This urge to do everything all at once is often driven by a combination of factors connected to a strong personal sense for achievement, pride of ownership as a small business owner, or the robust sales benchmarks insurance companies assess on agents in order for them to maintain their sales contracts and recognition programs.

The truth be known, it is a singular impossibility for any individual in any undertaking to do everything all at one time. Success takes planning, deliberate execution, and a building block approach, especially when building a high-performing and highly productive agency.

DON'T FEEL AS IF YOU HAVE TO ACCOMPLISH THE IMPOSSIBLE AS AN AGENT

Allow the inertia of a simple plan of growth with planned dates for implementation of specific marketing systems to carry you to success. Resist the temptation to 'boil the ocean'; that is, do not allow yourself to succumb to the destructive effects of being overwhelmed by all that has to be done as an agent or business owner.

Be realistic. Yes, there is a lot to running an agency and to selling the greatest product ever conceived by the mind of man, but don't be overwhelmed by the enormous size of the task before you. Divide your energy and attention into three predominant categories.

AGENT-OWNERSHIP REVOLVES AROUND THREE MAJOR AREAS: THE ORGANIZATION, MARKETING & SALES

The Organization: This area of small business ownership is about the systemic structure, health, and efficiency of the organization itself.

This is an area of business ownership that can cause a lot of frustration and worry for someone. In regard to an agent-owner selling insurance and financial services products, the exact way in which an office is structured can vary quite a bit.

How staff is organized, how pay is distributed and earned, how roles are defined, and how business is transacted is as diverse as it is daunting when it comes to the man-hours dedicated to running an effective organization.

The following eight principles represent the key elements of an effective sales organization:

1. Manage to Performance/Behaviors. Avoid employee resentment and discontentment by keeping performance-based discussions focused on actions and results as much as is possible. Do not personalize your performance appraisals and estimates of your employees.

2. Do not bestow privileges or rewards upon anyone without them taking upon requisite responsibility. In turn, do not

place responsibility upon your employees without the requisite privilege or reward in return. Privilege and responsibility should never be separate matters. They are inextricably tied together as one idea, one concept, and one principle of employee management.

3. The closer you can place the power or ability to fix problems and make decisions to customer-facing levels, the more efficient and effective the organization. Empower your customer-facing employees to make decisions on behalf of customers and the business organization, but do not grant this privilege without an employee first proving they will be responsible with that power.

4. Profit is not the prime directive in running a business. As Peter Drucker, business expert and author has often stated, the sole reason for business existence is to "create a customer." Don't put the cart before the horse. Realize that if all your organizational activities are designed to create a customer—that is, to draw their attention, loyalty, and patronage to your business—the profits will naturally follow as a result. As the old saying goes, "If we build it, they will come." If you build processes that will attract and create customers, the sales will come.

5. Cash flow is king when it comes to running any business. It is a two-sided coin. On one side, a business must develop as many revenue streams as possible. On the other side of the cash flow coin, expense management is just as important. Expense management is about simplicity and discipline. Simplicity in that a business owner should not spend money on anything that doesn't have to do with marketing, sales, or the organizational support of those two functions. When it comes to discipline, it takes a disciplined individual to adhere to such a simple plan as I have proposed.

6. Where personal investment is lacking, so will there be a lack of commitment to success or excellence. Unless a person is invested either by way of time, money, or ideas, there will be no

commitment on their part to the success of the organization. For the agent-owner, use regular team meetings and other forums to foster employee investment into the agency. Oftentimes, the best and easiest way to get people invested is by soliciting their ideas on how to improve the business operation.

7. People rise to the level of expectation you have in them. Encourage and equip your employees for success. Establish specific roles and boundaries for them to operate within during business hours. Partner with your employees in establishing work goals. Make sure your expectations of them are clearly understood and that they indicate a realistic belief you have in their abilities and capabilities to be successful.

8. Create an environment that is marketing and sales oriented. All processes and procedures adopted by the organization should ultimately be focused on getting people in front of a sales professional. All other activities are secondary in priority.

Marketing: As I define it, marketing is all those things we do to get and keep customers. It is an area of small business ownership that can often be the most difficult. Why? Because marketing is about getting and keeping customers. It involves action, movement, execution, and persistency—not to mention a lot of patience at times.

It is the block-and-tackle part of the sales business, the foundational work from which all sales results are born. Without the hard work of marketing, nothing—absolutely nothing—gets done for the insurance agent.

The following seven principles will help in building effective marketing processes within an agency:

1. Focus the majority of your daily energy on the execution of specific marketing activities. Compared with selling, marketing involves a greater degree of effort in order to be successful. Once a prospect is face to face with a sales professional, the

Pull Your Nose Up

great majority of them will buy. Insurance agencies never fail because of a weak sales force or poor individual salesmanship. Agencies fail because of inadequate or ineffective marketing execution. The secret to sales success is no secret at all; having enough opportunities to conduct a sales conversation with people is what creates sales success. The only way that can be accomplished is through executing a marketing plan. Don't be distracted from the simple fact that marketing success is fueled by determined, consistent execution of a plan of marketing. Otherwise, it's just a plan and nothing more.

2. A solid marketing plan has *balance* within and without. It has balance in terms of mining business opportunities from *within* the book of business and *without* the book of business. That is, there is oftentimes a 'book within the book' when referring to additional sales to current customers. Take every opportunity available to you to cross-sell and even up-sell your current customer list. A lopsided marketing approach common to agents is to market their current customers almost exclusively at the sacrifice of marketing outside the book toward new ones. That is a mistake in terms of missed opportunities for growth and stability.

3. A solid marketing plan has *balance* in creating *awareness* and in creating *attraction*. By marketing awareness, I am referring to broad-based advertising such as billboards, radio and television ads, telephone book ads, fliers and posters, signs, and any other media designed more for market presence and identity rather than driving business to a specific storefront, website, or phone number. Be discriminate with your marketing budget. Have a presence in both marketing realms, but use the bulk of your marketing dollars on processes that specifically attract and drive business to your transaction portals be it a brick-and-mortar storefront, an Internet site or a 1-800 number. The desire to feel good about buying billboard space or telephone book ads should be tempered by the reality that these marketing mediums do little in terms of creating an acceptable return on investment for the insurance agent trying to grow his/her business.

4. A solid marketing plan has balance between *passive* processes and *active* processes. The idea of passive and active processes fits well with our previous discussion about awareness and attraction. Many marketing awareness efforts are not efforts at all. They tend to be passive attempts at getting people in front of you. A billboard, for instance, is an extremely popular, yet passive means of marketing. Many agents use billboards to market themselves, and sadly, many more use billboards and other passive methods as their primary means for marketing. These methods tend to be expensive, difficult to measure in terms of return on investment and simply not productive when it comes to the predictable efforts of more active means of marketing. I will not discount the importance of billboard advertising and other passive-awareness methods in an overall, well-balanced marketing strategy. What I will discount is the effectiveness of such advertising over more active methods such as cold calling and other telemarketing, leveraging centers of influence and other relationships, and participating in civic and community events in order to drive customers to your storefront.

5. An effective marketing plan is repeatable. It is a process whereby the individual tasks required to execute the process in its entirety can be repeated week in and week out as a productive activity.

6. An effective marketing plan is also layered in its processes that take advantage of near-term, intermediate, and long-term sales opportunities. A near-term process may be a weekly proactive telemarketing activity that targets new home owners for mortgage protection and new car ownership. An intermediate process might be an activity that capitalizes on small business ownership and the unique commercial insurance needs of that market segment. And finally, a long-term marketing effort may be either large commercial and group accounts or a coordinated direct mail campaign involving a deliberate mailing and telemarketing effort tied together to create

multiple customer 'touches' in order to win their patronage as a new customer.

7. An effective marketing plan is written down.

Sales: If marketing is all those things we do to get people in front of us and to create a loyal customer base at the same time, *sales* is what we do in front of people.

The selling function is a natural transition away from the work and science of marketing to the art and craft of persuasion.

Selling is movement, connection, nuance, awareness, intuition, structure, performance, balance, timing, subtlety and empathy — all these things and more.

Sales is a contact sport! It's theater, a stage on which persuasion is born.

Selling is about technique. It is the art of persuasion as much as it is science in communication. It is fueled by marketing and steered by individual skill.

Selling is also a perishable skill that degrades and wanes with each day an individual is away from the practice of selling.

Therefore, refining your selling skills by way of scripting, role play, videotape feedback, and other methods is imperative to improving on one's closing ratio and in maintaining high performance as a professional.

Selling is about technical knowledge and being able to know and articulate the details of a product or service in language the customer will understand and appreciate.

Selling is theater that calls upon our skills as players expressing in the most convincing and believable manner why someone should choose us to buy a particular thing.

Selling is connection: a bond, common ground, emotion, intuition, and an urge that is created and felt between buyer and seller that points to trust and confidence among individuals. It is the point at which value is communicated by the agent and received and understood by the customer.

Selling, the skill that takes a person from prospect and possibility to client and loyal supporter, is among the most important business skills to acquire. Of the following critical metrics that directly impact revenue for an agency:

1. The number of prospects/leads generated (marketing) on a consistent basis
2. The average earned premium generated per sale
3. The number of transactions/sales per household or individual
4. The margin set by the company (commissions) for each sale. For most agents, this is a metric, or element of revenue, that cannot be negotiated or controlled directly by the agent. The company often sets the margin on the products agents sell with little to no input on the part of their sales force, but what agencies and agents can do in order to amplify or increase the effects of established company margins is to keep expenses as low as possible. This is a unique element of the average agency business model versus most other small business ventures.
5. Retention of customers already sold and the residual income it produces.
6. The number of prospects turned into customers (closing ratio) for a typical insurance agency operation.

Selling, or the closing ratio, is the one factor that can produce the greatest proportionate impact on revenue and profit for the business owner when compared to the other four elements that directly impact revenue.

Improving on an individual's or agency's ability and skill to close more sales (closing ratio) given a defined number of leads is usually the most cost effective means to increased revenue for a business entity.

THE CLOSING RATIO IS QUEEN

If cash flow is king, as I previously stated in this chapter, then selling, or the closing ratio, is queen. Stay focused on what matters to your agency and keep it simple as a business owner. Resist the urge to do everything. Keep to the basics and be flawless at the essentials when it comes to running an agency.

In the game of football, blocking, tackling, running, and passing the ball are the basic building blocks of the sport. Beyond these basic skills, there isn't much to the game that the mind can further conceive. Thus, winning is a simple task of mastering these basics and nothing more.

In our profession, the selling of insurance and financial services products has become too complicated a task for many sales professionals. Our great need is to embrace simplicity, to keep things simple and practice delivering sales conversations that our customers understand.

Like football, in which the team that blocks best, tackles best, runs best, and passes the football best is usually the winner, the agent or agency that runs an effective *organization* best, *markets* best, and *sells* best will be the winner.

It doesn't get any more complicated than that.

Be great at the basics. Focus on what is important to success and don't try to boil the ocean. In time, you will eventually put in place all the systems you envision for success. Do not let impatience spoil your journey to success. You will get there… one step at a time.

About the Author

With over twenty-six years of military and corporate working experience, along with sales, marketing, and business ownership to his credit, Tony has made it his life mission to share with people the personal lessons of success and the setbacks he has witnessed and lived in order to help others achieve their dreams in life. Two areas he focuses his attention on are small business ownership success—particularly as it relates to those in the insurance and financial services industry—and individual development and advancement.

A veteran of the Air Force and Distinguished Graduate of the USAF Fighter Weapons School and Gulf War Veteran, Tony has worked with hundreds of agent-owners and sales professionals, helping them to improve their bottom- line results of increased income and production results. He has been a sought-after group speaker and consultant for individuals looking to navigate the corporate waters and marketplace in order to achieve their career goals.

He is a motivator of people and innovator in developing and delivering sales and marketing curriculum for some of the largest insurance companies in America. Tony holds a B.S. from Rochester Institute of Technology and has his M.A. and M.S. degrees from Troy State University and Bethany Theological Seminary in Alabama.

An eighteen-year veteran of the insurance and financial services

Anthony D. Cefalu

industry, he has an associates in claims (AIC) designation and holds the professional designation of CLU. He is also the author of the book, *Sales Is a Contact Sport*, used by sales organizations and business groups.

Tony is the founder of Transformation Systems Group and the Executive Vice President of Career Advisors Group, both partnerships of consultants and experts dedicated to the development of individuals, small businesses, and organizations looking to discover new capabilities, seize opportunities, and realize their dreams of success.

Currently, he works for a Fortune 500 insurance and financial services company based in Ohio.

www.ingramcontent.com/pod-product-compliance
Lightning Source LLC
Chambersburg PA
CBHW031833170526
45157CB00001B/287